A Letter
from the Adherents of the Sunnah of Our Beloved
Prophet Muhammad (sws)
to the Shia

﴿إِنَّ الَّذِينَ فَرَّقُوا دِينَهُمْ وَكَانُوا شِيَعًا لَسْتَ مِنْهُمْ فِي شَيْءٍ إِنَّمَا أَمْرُهُمْ إِلَى اللَّهِ ثُمَّ يُنَبِّئُهُمْ بِمَا كَانُوا يَفْعَلُونَ﴾

{Verily, those who divide their religion and break up into sects, you have no concern in them in the least. Their affair is only with Allah, Who then will tell them what they used to do.}[Al-An`aam 6: 159]

A partial selection of the erroneous beliefs and false allegations of this sect, with an explanation of why they are incorrect, followed by a brief, but unequivocal rebuttal of each

Compilation:
Muhammad al-Sayed Muhammad

Table of Contents

Introduction	4
The founder of the Shia sect and the beginnings of its emergence	5
Shia beliefs about Allah the Creator and why these are incorrect	6
Shia beliefs about the Angels and why these beliefs are incorrect	8
Shia beliefs about the Holy Quran and why these are incorrect	10
Examples of things ascribed to Prophet Muhammad (sws) and believed about him and why these claims and beliefs are both reprehensible and incorrect	12
The Shia belief about the wives of Prophet Muhammad (sws) and why it is incorrect	17
The Shia belief about the companions of Prophet Muhammad (sws) and why it is incorrect	21
The Shia belief about drawing near to Allah Almighty by insulting and cursing honorable members of the Prophet's (sws) household and why it is incorrect	27
The Shia beliefs about the Imams and the Doctrine of *Bada'* (New Decision), and why these are incorrect	29
The Shia beliefs about Succession and Revelation after the prophet Muhammad (sws), and why these are incorrect	32
The Shia belief in *Raja'* (Resurrection), a brief refutation of this claim and an explanation of why it is incorrect	35
The Shia position on graves, and therefore, association of partners with Allah Almighty	37

The Shia's glorification of those in the graves, seeking help from them, and taking them as intercessors with Allah Almighty	39
The Shia and their (illegitimate) seeking of blessing, plus their belief that others besides Allah can benefit them	40
Practical examples of the heretical beliefs of the Shia	42
Religious rituals of the Shia	43
The Doctrine of the Clay in which the Shia believe, a brief refutation of it and an explanation of why it is incorrect	44
The Shia belief about Karbala, and why it is incorrect	47
The Shia belief about the Mahdi	49
What the Shia Mahdi will supposedly do, with refutation	50
Dire warnings about the Shia belief in the Imamate, in general, and the twelfth Imam whose emergence from hiding is awaited, in particular	54
The Mahdi according to the followers of Prophet Muhammad's (sws) Sunnah	55
Shia beliefs, summarized	57
The Shia and the legalization of prostitution (*muta'* marriage), with refutation	58
The Shia belief about *Khums* (the official share of the spoils of war), and why it is incorrect	62
Contradictions about the Shia (and those of their ilk)	63
Similarities between the Shia and the Jews and the Shia and the Christians	71
How the Jews and Christians are better than the Shia	73

Those Allah Almighty has guided to the Way of the Best of all People, Muhammad (sws) and the followers of *Ahl ul-Sunnah*	74
Doubts and misconceptions stirred up by the Shia, with brief refutation	75
Falsehood and its many faces, and how they ally with one another	89
A letter from the adherents of the Sunnah of the beloved, Prophet Muhammad (sws), to the Shia	91
Conclusion	93

Introduction

All praise is due to Allah, Lord of the Worlds, Maker of the heavens and earth, Bringer of darknesses and Light. I bear witness that there is none worthy of worship beside Allah, Alone, Who is without partner, and I bear witness that Muhammad, *salla Allahu alaihi wa sallam* (sws: peace and blessings be upon him), is His slave and messenger.

Oh Allah, praise, extol, and bless Prophet Muhammad, the Seal of the Prophets and Messengers. Oh Allah, praise, extol, and bless the pure and righteous members of his household, his noble companions, and those who align themselves with his guidance, follow his way, and walk in his footsteps until the Day of Judgment.

To proceed:

Long ago, there emerged a sect distinguishing between Prophet Muhammad's (sws) wives and the members of his family. In fact, they attacked them and slandered them, besides declaring them disbelievers, as they also did to the Prophet's (sws) Companions, in addition to their many other false beliefs, the likes of which no Jew, Christian, or other adherent of false beliefs would deign to accept. This sect of which we speak—the Shia (the Partisans of Ali and those of their kind)—believe that their Scripture (the Holy Quran) which they admit and confess descended upon Prophet Muhammad (sws) through revelation from above has been changed. And this is only the beginning.

The sect to which we refer—the Shia and those like them—are also called the Twelvers.

This brief, concise presentation of my research will—Allah willing—address some of the erroneous beliefs and false claims of this sect, it will clarify why they are incorrect and it will provide an unequivocal refutation of them.

Before the reader begins to read this research, we would ask that he rid himself before Allah Almighty of any fanaticism, partisanship, or nationalism...this before all else.

He should not let his reading of this research be that of vilification, fault-finding and discrediting because that is no benefit, and he will take truth to be falsehood without examining it critically or contemplating it.

Therefore, the reader should proceed as a seeker of truth who wishes only to follow it and to propagate it, not to discredit it and lead others away from it.

Let the esteemed reader remember the Bounty of Allah Almighty upon him that He set the truth before his eyes to think upon it and contemplate it. He did not keep it hidden.

We ask Allah (Glorious & Exalted) to give our words effect and to guide through us the hearts of His slaves, so that when they read this, it will really hit their hearts, so that they will respond and benefit from it.

We ask Him (Mighty & Sublime) to grant us acceptance in this world and the Next, to guide us and guide others through us and make us a cause of their guidance, for He (Glorious & Exalted) is the Only One with the Authority over that and the Only One Capable of it.

The Founder of the Shia Sect and the Beginnings of Its Emergence

Shiism was established on corrupt, untrue principles, concocted by Abdullah ibn Saba', the Jew, who is considered the founder of this renegade sect, when he claimed divinity for Ali ibn Abi Talib, in exchange for being made a prophet.

It is for that reason that Ibn Saba', the Jew, claimed to be a prophet (may Allah curse him).

In the glaring face of this fact, we find that the Shia have tried to escape it in a number of different ways: by denying it from the lips of their clerics and by claiming that Abdullah ibn Saba', the Jew, is an imaginary character, to evade the truth and to display arrogance towards those who follow it.

However, the attempts by the Shia to deny this fact have all met with failure, and this is due to the clear passages contained in many authoritative sources.

Among the sources upon which the Shia rely, which contain record of that which would expose them in this matter, are: *Al-Anwar al-Na`maniyyah* (2/34), by Ni`amatullah al-Jaza'iriyy al-Shi`iyy, *Al-Maqalat wal-Firaq*, by al-Qimmiyy, and also *Rijaal al-Kishiyy*, by al-Kishiyy, and more.

In these sources, it is clear that the person of Abdullah ibn Saba', the Jew, is real; he is not imaginary as the Shia like to claim in order to avoid the lifting of the mask and the scandal they think they have buried and covered up.

Therefore, the beginnings of Shiism and its emergence at the hand of that Jew, Abdullah ibn Saba', the Jew, also known as Ibn Sawdaa', who appeared to follow Islam while hiding his disbelief, and who claimed that it is written in the Torah that every prophet has a successor (*wasiyy*) and that Ali (may Allah be pleased with him) was the successor of Muhammad (sws).

Then the Jew, Ibn Saba', claimed that Ali (may Allah be pleased with him) was divine, claiming for himself prophethood, and those who were deceived into believing Ibn Saba's claim were called Saba'iya, after Ibn Saba', the founder of the Shia sect.

And so Shiism as we see it today was invented, with its false claims and its reprehensible doctrines that no one of pure nature or sound mind could ever accept.

All praise is due to Allah Almighty for the blessing of Islam, and all praise is due to Him for the gift of guidance and righteousness.

Shia Beliefs about Allah the Creator
and Why These Are Incorrect

Allah (Mighty & Majestic) is God, the Creator of all living beings, including human beings, and He has given them more blessings than can be counted or enumerated. One of the most important of these is the blessing of the mind, with which he may ponder the wonders of Allah's creations (may He be glorified and exalted), the greatness of His Power, the perfection of His Handiwork, and the extent of His Knowledge and Wisdom...as well as all the other Beautiful Attributes of Allah (Blessed & Exalted), so as to glorify Him and proclaim His Greatness.

However, we find that there are people who handle this tool poorly and do not use it well. In fact, there are those who make their reason follow their base whims and that which their egos desire, without bringing to bear the faculty of reason, thought, and contemplation.

Among those who have used the mind poorly, denying for it the gift of reason, are the Shia. This renegade sect have denied this great blessing—the blessing of reason—and employed it poorly, which has led them to cast aspersions on their God, to ascribe that which is defamatory to Him, and to attribute impairment to Him. The proof of this is in the doctrines of the Shia about Allah (Glorious & Exalted): at their inception, they believed in incarnation—the Divine taking physical form—upon their initial establishment at the hand of Abdullah ibn Saba', the Jew, in their description of Allah Almighty.

May Allah be exalted high above such a saying!

Afterwards, the Shia became Jahmiyyah and Mu`attilah (deniers of the Divine Attributes), for they chose to describe Allah (Glorious & Exalted) with attributes of imperfection and deprivation. This is absolutely clear in the narrations they regularly refer to, among which are:

That which was narrated by Ibn Babawaih, the Shiite, in more than 70 narrations, which say that Allah Almighty "cannot be described by time or place, nor by condition, movement or travel, and not by the descriptors of bodies, neither sensory, nor corporeal, nor image." (*Al-Tawhid*, by Ibn Babawaih)

And so the Shia clerics have continued in this misguided way, denying the attributes affirmed by the Quran and Sunnah.[1]

All of this runs contrary to the clear verses of the Book of Allah (Mighty & Majestic): the Holy Quran. It also contradicts the authentic, authoritative sayings of Allah's chosen, trustworthy messenger, Muhammad (sws). In fact, it even goes against sound logic; indeed, it directly contradicts it.

And the proof is:

If we wished to describe something nonexistent (the void: that which has no being), we would not be able to describe it more than that.

Is God, the Creator (Glorious & Exalted) nonexistent—that which is without being?

Can anyone of sound nature and pure soul, with a discriminating, rightly-guided intellect accept the likes of such nonsense (as the claims of the Shia) concerning the Divine Creator (Glorious & Exalted)?

Of course not.

May Allah (Mighty & Majestic) be exalted above everything the Shia and others have made up!

---

[1] From *Kitab `Aqaa'id al-Shi`ah* (with minor editing), by Abdullah ibn Muhammad al-Salafiy

The correct belief which concurs with sound nature and pure souls, which the discriminating, rightly-guided intellect accepts is: affirmation of that which Allah Almighty has affirmed for Himself, from the Attributes mentioned in His Perfect Book, the Holy Quran, or from the lips of His trustworthy messenger, Muhammad (sws), without denial, alteration, or interpretation, and without anthropomorphism or asking how.

This stays within the confines of the Saying of Allah (Glorious & Exalted),

﴿لَيْسَ كَمِثْلِهِ شَيْءٌ وَهُوَ السَّمِيعُ الْبَصِيرُ﴾

It means, {**There is nothing like unto Him**}. [Al-Shura 42: 11]

Everything that comes to our minds, Allah (Glorified & Exalted) is other than it, for He (Glorified & Exalted) is More Magnificent and More Exalted than that. No mere human mind can imagine the Glorious Attributes of Allah, the Supreme Creator. This is what the adherents of the Sunnah of the beloved prophet, Muhammad (sws), profess to believe.

As a result, we see that the creed of the adherents of the Sunnah of the beloved prophet, Muhammad (sws), is the clear, pure creed, unsullied by flaw or ambiguity.

And all praise is due to Allah Almighty for the blessing of Islam, and all praise is due to Him for the gift of guidance and righteousness.

Among that which the Shia have perpetrated against the Rights of Allah are:

The Shia negated Allah's Omniscience—His All-Encompassing, Perfect Knowledge—and as such, they have slandered His Perfect Wisdom and Perfect Power...and so on of the Attributes of Allah Almighty, under the heading of what they call the Doctrine of *Bada'* (New Decision).

According to this belief, the Shia claim that Allah Almighty can, supposedly, 'change His mind,' meaning that He was going to make something happen in the future and He willed it, but then something else occurred to Him (*bada'* means: to appear after being hidden), so He goes back on what He originally intended to do (because He now sees the error therein or the lack of choosing the better option thereby).

May Allah (Mighty & Majestic) be exalted high above the likes of such slander!

This is without a doubt a clear impugnation of Allah, the Creator (Glorious & Exalted) and an attribution of imperfection to Him.

Allah Almighty is the All-Knowing, whose Knowledge completely encompasses all things. He (Glorious & Exalted) knows the visible and the invisible. He knows what was, what is, and what will be. He also knows if something were to be, how it would be.

Allah (Glorious & Exalted) is not incapable of anything. Nothing keeps Him busy from anything else. He is the Creator of something from nothing. There is none like unto Him. May He be glorified and exalted! It is inconceivable that He could make a mistake or fail to do what is better, since it is part of His Perfect Wisdom that He does not do anything but what is best. Just as Allah Almighty has the Perfect Attributes, He (Glorious & Exalted) only performs Perfect Acts.

This is the clear, pure creed professed by the adherents of the beloved prophet, Muhammad (sws). It is untainted by the slightest flaw and it is unsullied by the slightest ambiguity.

Other than what we have here presented in brief are a multitude of aspersions cast by the Shia's beliefs upon Allah Himself (Glorious & Exalted), impairments ascribed to His Most Beautiful Attributes, and detractions from His Perfection.

May Allah (Mighty & Majestic) be exalted high above that which the Shia invent about Him!

And all praise is due to Allah Almighty for the blessing of Islam, and all praise is due to Him for the gift of guidance and righteousness.

Shia Beliefs about the Angels
and Why These Beliefs are Incorrect

To begin, we would like to note the fact that:
It is not possible in any way to believe that any wrong could come from any of Allah Almighty's angels, nor is it possible to entertain the possibility, or to believe that they could fall short in what they were ordered to do or what they were made responsible for by Him (Glorious & Exalted). That is because the angels were not created by Allah Almighty with the ability to choose between good and bad (like the *jinn* and man); they were created with the nature to obey Allah Almighty and to carry out His Orders, according to His Intentions (Glorious & Exalted), His Will, and His Ultimate Wisdom.

If what we just stated is particular to angels in a general sense, what are we to think about those who were chosen by Allah (Glorious & Exalted) to be His closest angels or those Allah Almighty selected for the most noble, glorious and magnificent missions, which are: the Revelation (Allah Almighty's Words, Decrees, and Commandments) to the prophets and messengers who invite others to the worship of Allah Almighty?

As such, to impugn any of them, especially the most noble of them, and those chosen by Allah Almighty to bring down the revelation, and to believe them capable of error or shortcoming in what they were ordered to do by the Almighty, this in itself is to impugn Allah Himself (Glorious & Exalted), it is to detract from the Perfection of His Handiwork, and it is to attribute impairment to it.

In other words, anyone who believes any error or shortcoming could proceed from the angels of Allah Almighty (especially the chosen ones), in whose nature it is to obey and carry out His Orders, is thereby saying, even if only by implication, that Allah is not capable of perfecting His Handiwork or carrying out His Will enough to create the angels in the way He wills. May Allah (Mighty & Majestic) be exalted above such an idea!

As a result, the belief that any of the angels could make a mistake or fall short of their duty is an affront against the Will of Allah (Glorious & Exalted), as is the claim that He brings into being in His Dominion and from among His Creations that which is contrary to His Intent and Will. It is therefore a negation of His Wisdom, implying a lack of Complete Power...in addition to the other attributes of which it implies imperfection in Allah Himself (Glorious & Exalted), due to the slander initiated by what the Shia claim because of this corrupt belief.

What are we to think when the one who is impugned and accused of error and shortcoming is one of the closest of Allah's angels, indeed, the most honored of them, whom Allah Almighty elected and commanded to carry down the Revelation from Him (Glorious & Exalted) upon His prophets and messengers—the Angel Gabriel (peace be upon him), the one entrusted with the revelation from on high?

The Shia claim that the Angel Gabriel (peace be upon him) has fallen short in his duty to his Lord. They believe that he made a mistake by bringing down the message to Prophet Muhammad (sws) instead of bringing it down upon Ali (may Allah be pleased with him), his paternal cousin, the son of his uncle, Abu Talib.

In fact, there are certain sects of the Shia who say that the Angel Gabriel (peace be upon him) is guilty of betrayal for bringing the Revelation to Prophet Muhammad (sws) instead of bringing it to his cousin, Ali ibn Abi Talib (may Allah be pleased with him).

Undoubtedly, this is all nonsense; it could never make sense to anyone of sound mind, pure soul, or discriminating, rightly-guided intellect.

Besides the fact that whoever believes it is possible for any of the Almighty's angels to commit an error or experience a shortcoming, especially the closest of them to Allah, and indeed the most honored and esteemed of them, in what he has been commanded by Allah Almighty, and contradicted the nature with which he was created, which is to carry out His Commands, then this means that he could have made a mistake or fallen short in anything other than his duties, many, many times, for there would be no limits to this under such circumstances.

Were the situation as such, concerning he who was chosen by Allah Almighty to bring down the Revelation from Him to His prophets and messengers, then what about the other angels who are lesser (lower than the Angel of Revelation, who was entrusted to bring Allah's message to the prophets and messengers: the Angel Gabriel, peace be upon him), in station and esteem than him, or in standing and position (while maintaining their high position and elevated status before Allah Almighty)?!!

If that were the case, then these lesser angels would also necessarily have fallen into error or shortcoming because, if one more honored than them in station and status (the Angel Gabriel, peace be upon him) was not safe from this, would they be safe from it (in conformity with Shia beliefs in the mistakes and shortcomings of the Angel Gabriel, peace be upon him)?!

Without a doubt, believing this false doctrine, which the Shia made up at the hands of their founder as one of many means of impugning Islam, leads to a host of evil deeds and leaves the door wide open to impugning Allah Himself (Glorious & Exalted), finding impairment in His Will and Intent, His Wisdom and Power.

This would then cast aspersions on His (Glorious & Exalted) Messages, as well as His prophets and messengers. It would cause denial of the Revelation He sent down upon them from above, both commands and prohibitions, rituals and laws, which is what no one of sound nature or pure soul would accept.

And what is all of this but a clear contradiction to the rightly-guided, sound mind? What is it but a clash with the lowest level of reason and bewilderment concerning its requirements?

Despite the sampling of corruption we have shown would result from this belief (that any of the angels could make a mistake or fall short in their duties to Allah Almighty), we find that the Shia believe it. Indeed, they make it one of their central tenets—one of the firm foundations of their sect.

As a result, the truth to which the adherents of the Sunnah of the beloved prophet, Muhammad (sws), cling becomes clear: belief in the infallibility of the angels of the Most Beneficent (Glorious & Exalted) from shortcoming or error in what they have been commanded to do. This is because of the nature with which they were created: to obey Allah (Glorious & Exalted) and carry out His Commands.

This is what sound nature, pure souls, and wise minds accept and agree upon.

And all praise is due to Allah Almighty for the blessing of Islam, and all praise is due to Him for the gift of guidance and righteousness.

Shia Beliefs about the Holy Quran
and Why These Are Incorrect

The Shia have claimed that the Quran we have in our hands today is not the Quran which was sent down upon Prophet Muhammad (sws). They say it has been corrupted, after being altered and changed.

This claim is undoubtedly false; in fact, it contradicts the Saying of Allah Most High,

﴿إِنَّا نَحْنُ نَزَّلْنَا الذِّكْرَ وَإِنَّا لَهُ لَحَافِظُونَ﴾

It means, {**Verily We: It is We Who have sent down the Reminder** (the Quran) **and surely, We will guard it** (from corruption).} [Al-Hijr 15: 9]

And it is common knowledge that Prophet Muhammad (sws) is the Seal of the Prophets—the one by whom Allah Almighty finalized the line of prophets and messengers. Thus, there will be no prophet or messenger after him (sws).

As a result, there will not be any other Divine Scripture sent down after the revelation of the Holy Quran which Allah Almighty revealed to His prophet, Muhammad (sws).

As such, the Wisdom of Allah Almighty necessitates that this Final Holy Book be protected from any corruption, alteration, or change therein. It must remain preserved in its Divinely-Ordained form in order to guide mankind and to preserve the Message of all previous books.

It is this belief that anyone of sound nature can accept concerning the Divine Attributes of Allah (Glorious & Exalted) and His Perfect Wisdom; it is this belief, and this belief alone, which righteous minds can accept.

This is what the adherents of the Sunnah of the beloved prophet, Muhammad (sws), and the followers of his way believe, since it is the clear, pure creed.

Therefore, the claim made by the Shia, who say that the Holy Quran has been corrupted, is completely impossible for any rational mind to accept, under any circumstances.

To accept this claim would mean to cast aspersions on the Message of Prophet Muhammad (sws) and to deny that his is the Final Message. In fact, it would also impugn the Wisdom of Allah, the Creator (Glorious & Exalted).

For instance, how could the Divine Creator (Glorious & Exalted), the Omniscient and All-Wise, finalize all previous Revelation with the Message of Prophet Muhammad (sws) without His Protection (Glorious & Exalted) over it?

And how could the Divine Creator (Glorious & Exalted), the Omniscient and All-Wise seal all previous Divine Scriptures by sending down the Holy Quran without Protection from Him (Glorious & Exalted) over it, without taking care of it within the Divinely-Ordained Bounds for the guidance of humanity towards Him (Glorious & Exalted)?!!

Also, it is common knowledge that Revelation is only sent down upon the prophet and messengers of Allah Almighty, not to anyone else, no matter how great their Favor with Allah (Glorious & Exalted).

Allah Almighty supports His prophets and messengers with miracles and extraordinary feats to bear witness to the truth of their call and message, so that they might believe in the Revelation sent down amongst them from Allah Almighty, have faith in them and their Message (which resonates with sound human nature, pure souls and righteous minds), follow them, and accept the laws and injunctions with which they have come.

So, how do the Shia claim that there will be Revelation after Prophet Muhammad (sws), when he is the one by whom all previous messages were sealed? Indeed, by the

Revelation of the Holy Quran upon him, sws), all previous Divine Scriptures were finalized!!

Could anyone accept this claim of the Shia?!

Of course, not.

Revelation is not sent down upon anyone besides prophets and messengers; it is not sent down on righteous believers, even if there is nothing to prevent them from receiving certain privileged blessings (*karaamaat,* singular: *karaamah*) from Allah Almighty other than the miracles (*mu'jizaat*) specific to the messengers and prophets.

Here we should mention that:

In order to testify that a certain person has been granted such a privileged blessing from Allah Almighty and that what happened to him is not magic, is that the person (to whom the *karaamah* happened) is a righteous believer, who follows the guidance of Prophet Muhammad (sws) without substitution or alteration, that he is not coming with anything contrary to Islam or with baseless lies for which there is no evidence.

Following the above reference, we will summarize what has become clear and certain to us, in the following fashion:

Firstly, there is the fact that, with the death of a prophet or messenger, the Revelation from above ceases. Secondly, if the Message of this prophet and messenger was to seal the prophets and messengers before him and it was the Final Message to seal all previous Messages, and therefore the Divine Scripture sent down by Allah Almighty to him was the last Book to be sent down from above to preserve them, then it would be protected by Allah (Blessed & Exalted) within the Divinely-Ordained Confines to ultimately guide humanity, in accordance with the Saying of Allah Most High,

﴿إِنَّا نَحْنُ نَزَّلْنَا الذِّكْرَ وَإِنَّا لَهُ لَحَافِظُونَ﴾

It means, {**Verily We: It is We Who have sent down the Reminder** (the Quran) **and surely, We will guard it** (from corruption).}[Al-Hijr 15: 9]

This protection from Allah (Blessed & Exalted) over His Final Message and His Book to preserve all previous Books and to seal the Message is from His Perfect Wisdom (Glorious & Exalted).

This is what it is not possible for sound human nature, pure souls, and wise minds to deny or contradict under any circumstances.

In addition to the fact that any aspersion cast on the Words of the Divine Creator (Glorious & Exalted), Who sent down the Final Divine Book (the Holy Quran, after which there will be no Revelation of any other Divine Scripture), is a slanderous attack against the Attributes of Allah (Glorious & Exalted) and His Perfect and Ultimate Wisdom. It is an attack against His Will, Intent, and Power to protect the Book He vowed to protect, which will be followed by no other, new Divine Scripture.

As a final conclusion:

What the Shia claim and invent, by saying that the Holy Quran has been corrupted, is a false saying, a reprehensible concoction, and a fabricated claim, which it behooves no person of sound nature and wise mind to accept.

For all praise is due to Allah Almighty for the blessing of Islam and for making us among the adherents to the Sunnah of the best of all mankind, Muhammad (sws).

And all praise is due to Allah Almighty for the gift of guidance and righteousness.

Examples of Things Ascribed to Prophet Muhammad (sws) and Believed about Him and Why These Claims and Beliefs Are Both Reprehensible and Incorrect

The Shia (and those of their ilk) have ascribed to the Messenger of Allah (sws) such reprehensible sayings and actions that pure, noble souls recoil upon hearing them. Upright, sound natures are loathe to believe such things, and righteous, sound minds cannot accept them for the indignity and slander heaped upon him (sws). The following is but a sampling of examples that have come to light:

A. The examples that appear herein are only a part of the abominable things the Shia have ascribed to the Messenger of Allah (sws): Al-Kalini (the Shiite) reported in *al-Usool* from al-Kafi "that Jibreel (Gabriel) descended upon Muhammad (sws) and his household and said, 'Oh Muhammad, Allah brings you glad tidings of a baby boy who will be born to Fatima and murdered by your community after you.' So, he said, 'Oh Jibreel, and peace be upon my Lord, I have no need of a baby boy born to Fatima who will be murdered by my community after me.' So he ascended, and then came back down and said much the same, 'Oh Jibreel, and may peace be upon my Lord, I have no need of a baby boy born to Fatima who will be murdered by my community after me.' So Jibreel ascended into the heavens, and then came down and said, 'O Muhammad, your Lord greets you with peace that He will make among your descendants the *imamah* (leadership), *wilayah* (custodianship), and *wisayah* (succession).' So he replied, 'I am content [with that].' Then he sent word to Fatima that 'Allah brings you glad tidings of a baby boy who will be born to you and murdered by my community after me,' so she sent word back to him that 'I have no need of a baby who your community will murder after you.' Then, he sent word to her that Allah (Mighty & Majestic) has made among her descendants the *imamah*, *wilayah*, and *wisayah*, so she sent word to him that 'I am content [with that].' And so she carried him with hardship and bore him with hardship, but al-Hussain did not nurse from Fatima (peace be upon her) or from any other woman. He used to be brought to the Prophet (sws) who would put his thumb in his mouth, and he would suck from it that which would sustain him for two or three days."[2]

Among the questions one might raise to show the reprehensibility of the Shia saying such a thing about the Messenger of Allah (sws) and about his daughter, Fatima (may Allah be pleased with her), and thus its utter falseness, are:

1. Isn't the Prophet Muhammad (sws) the one whose integrity was attested to by his Lord (Blessed & Exalted) in His Saying,

﴿وَإِنَّكَ لَعَلَىٰ خُلُقٍ عَظِيمٍ﴾

It means, {**And verily, you** (Muhammad) **are on an exalted standard of character**} [Al-Qalam 68: 4]

as well as numerous other noble verses of the Holy Quran?!

Answer: Of course, it is.

2. Is there not in discontent with what Allah Almighty has ordained a lack of propriety with the Divine Creator (Glorious & Exalted), which carries the penalty of a major sin?!

---

[2] *Lillahi thumma lit-Taareekh* (*For Allah, and then for History*), by al-Sayyid Hussain al-Musawi

Answer: Of course, there is.

3. So how do the Shia ascribe to Prophet Muhammad (sws) discontent with what Allah (Glorious & Exalted) has ordained, especially after Allah Himself (Glorious & Exalted) sent the good news, when he (sws) is the one whose character his Lord (Blessed & Exalted) attests to in numerous verses of His Holy Book (the Quran)?!

4. Also, how can the Shia ascribe to Fatima (may Allah be pleased with her) discontent with what Allah (Glorious & Exalted) has ordained, when she is the daughter of the best of all those who have taught and raised children—Prophet Muhammad (sws)?!

5. Is there not in what the Shia claim an egregious attack against the Messenger of Allah (sws), a defamation of him, and therefore, a charge of inadequacy against the One Who chose and selected him to be a prophet and messenger, i.e. the Divine Creator (Glorious & Exalted)?!

Answer: Of course, there is.

6. Is there not in what the Shia claim an abominable accusation, degradation, and disparagement of Allah Almighty's choice for the Seal of His Prophets and Messengers?! Is this not clearly the belief that He (Glorious & Exalted) made a bad choice?!

Answer: Of course, it is.

7. Can Allah Almighty really be likened to this corrupt belief the Shia hold, and does His messenger, Muhammad (sws), really fit the disparaging description attributed to him by them?!

Answer: Of course not.

And one could go on raising questions that would clearly show the reprehensibility of what the Shia claim and believe, expose the extent of their insolence towards Allah Almighty and the Seal of His Prophets and Messengers, Muhammad (sws), and prove that Prophet Muhammad's (sws) daughter, Fatima (may Allah be pleased with her), is also not safe from them (the beliefs and claims of the Shia).

B. Also, among the examples that clarify some of the abominable sayings the Shia have attributed to Prophet Muhammad (sws) are: that the Shia narrate on the authority of the Commander of the Faithful, Ali: that he came to Allah's Messenger (sws) and his family when Abu Bakr and Umar were there, and said, "So I sat between him and Aisha, and Aisha said, 'Have you found nowhere but my thigh and the thigh of Allah's Messenger?' So he (supposedly) replied, 'Oh Aisha!'"[3] (*Al-Burhan fi Tafsir al-Quran*, 4/225)

Then he (supposedly) came one time and did not find a place [to sit], so Allah's Messenger (sws) pointed for him to sit behind him, while Aisha was standing behind him, dressed, so Ali (peace be upon him) came and sat between Allah's Messenger and Aisha, so she said, angrily, "Have you not found for your rear end a place besides my lap?" So, the Messenger of Allah got mad and (supposedly) said, "O Humairaa' (Little Red One), do not hurt me concerning my brother."[4] (*Kitab Sulaim ibn Qais*, p. 179)

---

[3] *Lillahi, Thumma lit-Taareekh (For Allah, Then for History)*, by al-Sayyid Hussain al-Musawi
[4] ibid.

One might also raise questions that would show the despicable nature of the Shia claims about the Prophet Muhammad (sws) and Ali ibn Abi Talib (may Allah be pleased with him):

1. Isn't Prophet Muhammad (sws) the one to whose integrity and good character his Lord (Blessed & Exalted) attested in His Saying,

$$\text{﴿وَإِنَّكَ لَعَلَى خُلُقٍ عَظِيمٍ﴾}$$

It means, {**And verily, you** (Muhammad) **are on an exalted standard of character**} [Al-Qalam 68: 4]

in addition to the other noble verses in the Holy Quran?!

Answer: Of course, he is.

2. Aren't modesty (*hayaa'*) and protective jealousy (*ghairah*) among the great virtues of the Prophet Muhammad (sws)?!

Answer: Of course, they are.

3. Is there not in the claims the Shia make about Prophet Muhammad (sws) an egregious attack and abominable slander against him, in saying that he did not object to Ali sitting between him and his wife, Aisha (may Allah be pleased with her), but rather (supposedly) said, "Oh Aisha!" and "Do not hurt me through my brother"?! Is this not a blatant attack against and denigration of his great character by describing him (sws) as immodest and lacking in protectiveness (which he, sws, praised in so many noble hadiths) over his wife?

Answer: Of course, it is.

4. Is there not in Shia claims a repugnant belief, and a denigration and slander of Allah Almighty's choice for the Seal of His Prophets and Messengers?! Is this not clearly the belief that He (Glorious & Exalted) did not choose well?! Does this not imply denial of the testimony Allah Almighty has made concerning Prophet Muhammad (sws) in His Saying (Glorious & Exalted),

$$\text{﴿وَإِاللَّهَ لَعَلَى خُلُقٍ عَظِيمٍ﴾}$$

It means, {**And verily, you** (Muhammad) **are on an exalted standard of character**}?!

5. Can Allah Almighty really be likened to this corrupt belief the Shia hold, and does His Messenger, Muhammad (sws), really fit the disparaging description attributed to him by them?!

Answer: Certainly not.

6. And was Ali ibn Abi Talib, one of the companions of Allah's Messenger (sws), his paternal cousin, and the fourth caliph to succeed him (after Abu Bakr, Umar, and Uthman, may Allah be pleased with them all) shameless and ill-mannered, such that he would sit between Prophet Muhammad (sws) and his wife (may Allah be pleased with her)—and insistently, at that—even after what Aisha (raa) said to him?!!

Answer: Certainly not.

Thus one might go on raising questions that show the atrociousness of what the Shia claim and believe, and that expose the extent of the defamation against Allah Almighty and against the Seal of His Prophets and Messengers, Muhammad (sws), such that even the companion and paternal cousin of Allah's Messenger (sws)—Ali, may Allah be pleased with him—is not safe from them.

C. Further examples that show some of the abominable acts the Shia attribute to Prophet Muhammad (sws) are: (The Shiite) al-Majlisi related that the Commander of the Faithful (Ali) said, "I traveled with the Messenger of Allah (may Allah send peace and blessings upon him and his household) when he had no other servant besides me. I had with me a blanket (he had none besides it), and he had with him Aisha. Allah's Messenger used to sleep between me and Aisha, and all three of us had no other blanket besides it. So, when he would rise to pray (the Night Prayer), he would depress the blanket in the middle with his hand between me and Aisha until the blanket would touch the bed beneath us."[5] (*Bihaar al-Anwaar*, 2/40)

Among the questions one might raise which would show the atrociousness of the acts ascribed by the Shia to Prophet Muhammad (sws) and to Ali (may Allah be pleased with him), and therefore their falseness, are:

1. Isn't Prophet Muhammad (sws) the one whose character Allah (Blessed & Exalted) praised in His Saying,

﴿وَإِنَّكَ لَعَلَى خُلُقٍ عَظِيمٍ﴾

It means, {**And verily, you** (Muhammad) **are on an exalted standard of character**}

as well as other noble verses of the Holy Quran?!

Answer: Of course, he is.

2. Aren't modesty and *ghairah* (a feeling of protectiveness over one's women) among the great virtues of Prophet Muhammad (sws)?!

Answer: Of course, they are.

3. Is there not in the Shia's insolence and in the horrendous allegations brought against Prophet Muhammad (sws)—that he rose from his bed and left his wife sleeping next to another person who was not her close male relative (*mahram*)—defamation of his great virtues and a disparagement of him, by describing him as shameless and unconcerned about being cuckolded (even though *ghairah*, or a sense of protectiveness over one's women, is one of the characteristics of a Muslim, let alone that it is one of the defining traits of the prophets and messengers of Allah Almighty)?!

Answer: Of course, there is.

4. Would Prophet Muhammad (sws) accept for someone other than a close male relative to sleep in his bed beside his wife, even if he (sws) separated them?!

Answer: Certainly not.

---

[5] *Lillahi, Thumma lit-Taareekh* (*For Allah, Then for History*), by al-Sayyid Hussain al-Musawi

5. Is there not in the abominable conviction contained in these Shia claims disparagement and defamation of Allah Almighty's choice for the Seal of His Prophets and Messengers and a clear belief in His (Glorious & Exalted) poor selection?! Is there not, in this, abject denial of what Allah Almighty has informed us when He extolled the virtues of His prophet, Muhammad (sws), in His Saying (Glorious & Exalted),

$$﴿وَإِنَّكَ لَعَلَى خُلُقٍ عَظِيمٍ﴾$$

It means, {**And verily, you** (Muhammad) **are on an exalted standard of character**}?!

Answer: Of course, there is.

6. Can Allah Almighty be likened to this corrupt belief as the Shia allege? Can His messenger (sws) be likened to the disparaging description ascribed to him by them?!

Answer: Certainly not.

7. Was Ali ibn Abi Talib, the companion of Allah's Messenger (sws), his paternal cousin, and the fourth caliph to succeed him (after Abu Bakr, Umar, and Uthman, may Allah be pleased with them all) shameless and ill-mannered, such that he would agree to sleep beside Allah's Messenger (sws) and his wife?!

Answer: Certainly not.

8. Was Ali ibn Abi Talib shameless and ill-mannered, such that he would not object to lying beside the wife of Allah's Messenger (sws) after Prophet Muhammad (sws) had risen from the bed, when Ali knew that the Prophet (sws) had done so?!

Answer: Certainly not.

To what conclusions do these provocative questions (and others) point?! And what unavoidable and unequivocal answers have been reached?!
Without a doubt, all of these questions clearly show the great calumny and corrupt beliefs of the Shia, and therefore, the falseness of their claims.
One could go on providing examples which show the corruption of the abominable allegations and false claims of the Shia as a result of their malicious plans, which is to plot against Islam and its adherents.
Thus, all praise is due to Allah Almighty for the blessing of Islam, and for making us among the adherents of the Sunnah of the beloved, trustworthy prophet, Muhammad (sws).
And all praise is due to Allah Almighty for the gift of guidance and righteousness.

The Shia Belief about the Wives of Prophet Muhammad (sws) and Why It Is Incorrect

Allah (Blessed & Exalted) chose His prophets and messengers from His creation to invite people to worship Him and to spread His message, and He honored them with this glorious station—the station of prophethood and messengership.

Despite the great effort the prophets and messengers of Allah Almighty put forth to invite the people to worship Him (Glorious & Exalted) and to provide them with guidance, many did not respond, and among the unresponsive multitudes was sometimes: a son (e.g., the son of Nuh/Noah, peace be upon him) or a wife (e.g., the wife of Prophet Lut/Lot, peace be upon him).

This is neither considered defamation of the prophets and messengers of Allah Almighty, nor a shortcoming on their part. It is not considered a defect in the effort they put into calling them to the worship of Allah Almighty. That is because guidance is in the Hand of Allah (Glorious & Exalted). He (Glorious & Exalted) knows best the hearts of His slaves. He knows best whom He has chosen to receive guidance and mercy, and therefore, His Good Pleasure and the gardens of Paradise.

However, when any of the wives of the prophets and messengers of Allah are accused of adultery (*zina*) and betraying the honor of their husbands (the prophets and messengers of Allah), the matter is not just that of a failing on the wives' part; indeed, it becomes an issue for their husbands as well, especially when it is a matter of honor.

This is the opposite of any other issue—even the issue of disbelief (*kufr*) (as we have just indicated). If one of the wives of the prophets became a disbeliever, this would not be considered defamation of the prophets themselves if they had not fallen short in delivering the message to them, for such disbelief is only a failing on the part of the individual who does it. It is a stain on that person and that person alone.

As a result, if the virtue of one of the wives of Allah's prophets and messengers is maligned and she is accused of betraying the honor of her husband, this is absolutely impossible to accept, since it contradicts the honor and nobility bestowed by Allah Almighty on His prophets and messengers.

This is because a necessary part of the honor and nobility granted by Allah Almighty to His prophets and messengers is that He safeguard their honor concerning their wives' virtue. It entails that He protect them in this and that He not allow any of these putrid vices or despicable scandals to reach them.

This is what sound human nature accepts, it is what pure souls incline towards, and it is what does not conflict with righteous minds.

Attacking the virtue of any of the wives of Allah Almighty's prophets and messengers is an attack against the prophets and messengers themselves. It is a denigration of them, and as such, it is a defamation of the Divine Creator (Glorious & Exalted) Himself, in that it implies that He chose unwisely who to honor with prophethood and messengership. May Allah (Mighty & Majestic) be exalted high above choosing His prophets and messengers unwisely! Indeed, He knows best whom to honor and raise to this most noble position and high station.

Allah (Glorious & Exalted) is the Divine Creator, Who possesses all the Attributes of Perfection in all their Glory and Beauty.

Despite all we have in this brief presentation, we find that the Shia have taken the path opposite to that which we have indicated. They have chosen a path that runs contrary to sound human nature and pure souls; it conflicts with proper reasoning. It contains gross disbelief in that which Allah Almighty revealed in His Perfect Book (the Holy Quran)—clear verses that will be recited until the coming of the Hour. Indeed, it contains complete rejection of that which has been established and authenticated as being from the Messenger of Allah (sws) in his noble prophetic traditions (*ahadith*).

Thus we find that the Shia attack the honor of Aisha (may Allah be pleased with her), the wife of Allah's Messenger (sws), the Mother of the Believers, and the daughter of Abu Bakr al-Siddiq. They have taken to insulting her and cursing her. In fact, they even call her a disbeliever, along with the other Mothers of the Believers—the wives of Allah's Messenger (sws)—showing special enmity towards her and her father. Likewise, they show particular enmity towards the Mother of the Believers, Hafsa, and her father, Umar ibn al-Khattab. This is in blatant denial of the noble verses revealed by Allah Almighty bearing witness to Aisha's innocence of that which the evil-doers accused her of. It is also in blatant denial of the noble verses that bear witness to their special status before Allah (Blessed & Exalted).

Additionally, this is denial and contradiction of the established, authentic hadiths from Prophet Muhammad (sws) which record the virtues of the Mothers of the Believers—the wives of Allah's Messenger (sws)—and their special status before Allah (Blessed & Exalted).

Among the noble verses which testify to the innocence of the Mother of the Believers, Aisha (may Allah be pleased with her), are what Allah Almighty sent down in Surat al-Nour, in the Words of Allah (Glorious & Exalted),

﴿إِنَّ الَّذِينَ جَاءُوا بِالْإِفْكِ عُصْبَةٌ مِنْكُمْ لَا تَحْسَبُوهُ شَرًّا لَكُمْ بَلْ هُوَ خَيْرٌ لَكُمْ لِكُلِّ امْرِئٍ مِنْهُمْ مَا اكْتَسَبَ مِنَ الْإِثْمِ وَالَّذِي تَوَلَّى كِبْرَهُ مِنْهُمْ لَهُ عَذَابٌ عَظِيمٌ * لَوْلَا إِذْ سَمِعْتُمُوهُ ظَنَّ الْمُؤْمِنُونَ وَالْمُؤْمِنَاتُ بِأَنْفُسِهِمْ خَيْرًا وَقَالُوا هَذَا إِفْكٌ مُبِينٌ * لَوْلَا جَاءُوا عَلَيْهِ بِأَرْبَعَةِ شُهَدَاءَ فَإِذْ لَمْ يَأْتُوا بِالشُّهَدَاءِ فَأُولَئِكَ عِنْدَ اللَّهِ هُمُ الْكَاذِبُونَ * وَلَوْلَا فَضْلُ اللَّهِ عَلَيْكُمْ وَرَحْمَتُهُ فِي الدُّنْيَا وَالْآخِرَةِ لَمَسَّكُمْ فِي مَا أَفَضْتُمْ فِيهِ عَذَابٌ عَظِيمٌ * إِذْ تَلَقَّوْنَهُ بِأَلْسِنَتِكُمْ وَتَقُولُونَ بِأَفْوَاهِكُمْ مَا لَيْسَ لَكُمْ بِهِ عِلْمٌ وَتَحْسَبُونَهُ هَيِّنًا وَهُوَ عِنْدَ اللَّهِ عَظِيمٌ * وَلَوْلَا إِذْ سَمِعْتُمُوهُ قُلْتُمْ مَا يَكُونُ لَنَا أَنْ نَتَكَلَّمَ بِهَذَا سُبْحَانَكَ هَذَا بُهْتَانٌ عَظِيمٌ * يَعِظُكُمُ اللَّهُ أَنْ تَعُودُوا لِمِثْلِهِ أَبَدًا إِنْ كُنْتُمْ مُؤْمِنِينَ * وَيُبَيِّنُ اللَّهُ لَكُمُ الْآيَاتِ وَاللَّهُ عَلِيمٌ حَكِيمٌ﴾

It means, {**Verily! Those who brought forth the slander** (against Aisha) **are a group among you. Consider it not a bad thing for you. Nay, it is good for you. Unto every man among them will be paid that which he had earned of the sin, and as for him among them who had the greater share therein, his will be a great torment. * Why then, did not the believers, men and women, when you heard it** (the slander) **think good of their own people and say, "This** (charge) **is an obvious lie?"* Why did they not produce four witnesses? Since they** (the slanderers) **produce not witnesses, they verily are liars in the Sight of Allah. * Had it not been for the Grace of Allah and His Mercy unto you in this world and in the Hereafter, a great torment would have touched you for that whereof you had spoken. * When you were propagating it with your tongues, and uttering with your mouths that whereof you had no knowledge, you counted it a little thing, while it was very great in the Sight of Allah. * And why did you not, when you heard it, say, "It is not right for us to speak of this. Glory be to You (O Allah)! This is a great lie"? * Allah forbids you from it and warns you not to repeat the likes of it forever, if you are believers. * And Allah makes the verses plain to you, and Allah is All-Knowing, All-Wise.**}
[Al-Nour 24: 11-18]

Among the noble verses which refer to Prophet Muhammad's (sws) wives—the Mothers of the Believers—and which therefore bear witness to their virtues and special status before Allah Almighty are His Saying (Glorious & Exalted),

﴿النَّبِيُّ أَوْلَىٰ بِالْمُؤْمِنِينَ مِنْ أَنْفُسِهِمْ وَأَزْوَاجُهُ أُمَّهَاتُهُمْ وَأُولُو الْأَرْحَامِ بَعْضُهُمْ أَوْلَىٰ بِبَعْضٍ فِي كِتَابِ اللَّهِ مِنَ الْمُؤْمِنِينَ وَالْمُهَاجِرِينَ إِلَّا أَنْ تَفْعَلُوا إِلَىٰ أَوْلِيَائِكُمْ مَعْرُوفًا كَانَ ذَٰلِكَ فِي الْكِتَابِ مَسْطُورًا﴾

It means, {**The Prophet is closer to the believers than their own selves, and his wives are their** (the believers') **mothers** (in respect to marriage and respect). **And blood relations among each other have closer personal ties in the Decree of Allah** (regarding inheritance) **than** (the brotherhood of) **the believers and the emigrants** (from Mecca), **except that you do kindness to those brothers** (when the Prophet, sws, joined them in ties of brotherhood). **This has been written in the Decrees** (Allah's Book of Divine Decrees).}
[Al-Ahzab 33: 6]

And there are other noble verses which refer to the virtues of the wives of the prophets, among whom are the wives of Prophet Muhammad (sws). As for the hadiths of Prophet Muhammad (sws) which show the virtues of the Mothers of the Believers (the wives of Allah's Messenger, sws), we refer the reader to the online encyclopedic resource, *al-Maktabah al-Shamilah*, because of its extensive collection of noble prophetic hadiths. This can be located by Internet search to learn more about the virtues of each of the wives of Prophet Muhammad (sws).

Here we would like to mention that in the noble verse contained in the Book of Allah Almighty, in His Saying (Glorious & Exalted),

﴿ضَرَبَ اللَّهُ مَثَلًا لِلَّذِينَ كَفَرُوا امْرَأَةَ نُوحٍ وَامْرَأَةَ لُوطٍ كَانَتَا تَحْتَ عَبْدَيْنِ مِنْ عِبَادِنَا صَالِحَيْنِ فَخَانَتَاهُمَا فَلَمْ يُغْنِيَا عَنْهُمَا مِنَ اللَّهِ شَيْئًا وَقِيلَ ادْخُلَا النَّارَ مَعَ الدَّاخِلِينَ﴾

{**Allah sets forth an example for those who disbelieve, the wife of Nuh (Noah) and the wife of Lut (Lot). They were under two of our righteous slaves, but they both betrayed their** (husbands by rejecting their doctrine), **so they** (Noah and Lot, peace be upon them both) **benefitted them** (their respective wives) **not against Allah, and it was said, "Enter the Fire along with those who enter!"**}
[Al-Tahrim 66: 10]

The point we would like to make is that His Saying (Glorious & Exalted), ﴿فَخَانَتَاهُمَا﴾ meaning, {**but they both betrayed them**}, does not refer to an adulterous betrayal; it refers to a betrayal of faith, meaning that the wife of Prophet Noah (peace be upon him) and the wife of Prophet Lot (peace be upon him) did not agree with their husbands (the prophets) on faith and they did not believe in the Message.[6]

The wife of Allah's prophet, Noah (peace be upon him), used to tell people he was crazy. Likewise, the wife of Allah's prophet, Lot (peace be upon him), used to lead her people to his guests.

As a result, as we have briefly shown before, we can clearly see that what the Shia have claimed and alleged concerning the Mothers of the Believers is a false allegation and reprehensible concoction. No one of sound human nature, pure soul, or righteous mind could accept it under any circumstances, let alone adopt it as religious doctrine.

Therefore, the truth is that which the adherents of the Sunnah of the beloved prophet, Muhammad (sws), have upheld—a clear, pure, sound belief about the wives of Prophet Muhammad (sws), the Mothers of the Believers, based on the evidence of Allah Almighty's Words in the Holy Quran and the hadiths of His prophet, the Greatest of the

---

[6] *Tafsir al-Quran al-Karim*, by Ibn Kathir

Messengers, Muhammad (sws), which concurs with sound human nature, pure, humble souls, and wise, righteous minds—namely: the belief in their special status before Allah Almighty, their superiority over the nation of Prophet Muhammad (sws) after him, and in their innocence from the accusations, allegations, and lies the Shia fabricate against them.

Thus, all praise is due to Allah Almighty for the blessing of Islam, and all praise is due to Him for the gift of reason. We thank Him for guiding us and showing us to His Straight Path and His Clear Way—the way of the adherents of the Sunnah of the beloved prophet, Muhammad (sws).

The Shia Belief about the Companions of Prophet Muhammad (sws) and Why It Is Incorrect

Before getting to the false and horribly audacious allegations the Shia have made up, we would like to make note of the following:

1. Just as believing in one of Allah Almighty's prophets makes more sense to the sound, righteous mind than denying him, believing in the goodness of whomever Allah Almighty has chosen to accompany, assist, and support His prophets, and to carry the flag after them—continuing their mission of calling people to Allah—makes more sense than to deny that the prophets' companions were good. This becomes particularly clear when we look at the Jews and Christians, since, despite their general disbelief, they still believe that the companions of the prophets were the best human beings after the prophets and messengers, and that is because Allah Almighty is the One Who chose them for this special position: the position of companionship.

Despite their errors, their quickness to show animosity toward the prophets and messengers, and their malice towards them, the Jews believe in the superiority of the prophets, and then the superiority of their companions. One example is that the Jews say that the companions of Musa/Moses were the best people of their religious community.

The Christians likewise say that Jesus' disciples were the best people in their religious community. We find that the adherents of the Sunnah of the beloved prophet, Muhammad (sws), have brought together the true monotheistic faith that the Jews and Christians have lost and the belief in the goodness of the companions of the prophets and messengers because of the favor they have been granted by Allah Almighty to be in this lofty position and high standing.

2. Believing in the Greatness, Beauty, and Perfection of Allah Almighty's Attributes requires belief in His (Blessed & Exalted) proper selection of those He has chosen to convey His message, and therefore, of His proper selection of whom to choose to assist them, support them, and carry the flag—calling the people to Allah—after them. It means belief in the wise selection of those who will lead the people after them and who will receive knowledge from them in order to teach it to the people after the prophets and messengers, because they are the ones who accompanied the prophets and messengers of Allah Almighty, learned from them and understood directly from them.

As such, it becomes clear that:

1. Allah Almighty's good selection of companions for His prophets and messengers is crucial for the preservation of the religion (Islam) they brought, for they will carry on the work of inviting people to it.

2. Belief in Allah Almighty's good selection of companions for His prophets and messengers—to assist and support them, carry on their work after them, and provide a good example for the people so that they can receive from them the religious knowledge they received from the prophets (since they are the ones who accompanied the prophets and messengers, learned from them, and understood from them)—is glorification of Allah Almighty and His High and Noble Attributes.

3. Belief in Allah Almighty's good selection of companions for His prophets and messengers is praise for them (the prophets and messengers), in that 'a person is on the religion of his closest friend' (the well-known Arabic axiom). The companions of the

prophets and messengers are, in effect, a mirror of them. In other words, belief in Allah Almighty's good selection of companions for the prophets and messengers is belief in Allah's good selection of the prophets and messengers, because the companions of the prophets and messengers (who will carry the flag of this religion after them) are of the same kind as those who responded to the call, followed their example, and trained at their hands.

As we have clearly seen, the belief in Allah Almighty's wise selection of companions for His prophets and messengers stands in stark contrast to the corrupt belief that the Almighty made a poor choice of companions for His prophets and messengers, and this in itself is:

1.   Disparagement of Allah (Glorious & Exalted), and defamation and diminishment of His High, Noble Attributes.

2.   Also, this corrupt belief in Allah Almighty's poor choice of companions for His prophets and messengers is a belief that the religion of Islam—which was sent down by Allah Almighty upon His prophets and messengers, to call the people to worship Him—is doomed to be lost and that it will not be preserved.

3.   In addition, this corrupt belief in Allah Almighty's poor choice of companions for His prophets and messengers is defamation and slander of those Allah Almighty chose to convey His message, because 'a person is on the religion of his closest friend.' In other words, the belief that the companions of the prophets and messengers are corrupt is a belief in the corruption of the prophets and messengers themselves. It is a slanderous accusation against them and an impugnation of their ability to preach, invite, and teach, and more, until those who hold such corrupt convictions and make such despicable allegations collapse into a closed loop of defaming the Divine Creator (Glorious & Exalted), diminishing His Status, and slandering Him for choosing poorly. And may Allah (Mighty & Majestic) be exalted high above choosing anything poorly!

Here are a few examples to illustrate the point:
If any of us saw a group of bad people and then he learned that these bad companions have a leader, what would we naturally think of the person claiming to be the leader of this bad group made up of evil individuals?
Undoubtedly, the first thing that would come to mind about the alleged leader of such a bad group would be that he must be the worst and most evil of them all because he is their leader.
And if the matter were otherwise, their alleged leader would be the opposite of the description of these bad people because they would adopt his manner and follow his lead, because they are from him and he is from them.

Therefore, from the little we have shown in brief and indicated, we can be sure that:
Belief in Allah Almighty's good selection of His prophets and messengers and those He (Blessed & Exalted) chose to accompany them, assist them, support them, and carry the flag of this religion after them, is an obligatory belief, required of every sane Muslim, who wants the truth, who does not follow vain desires, and who does not blindly follow those who came before him.

As a result, it is clear that:
1.   We are required to understand the differences that arose between the companions of the prophets and messengers of Allah Almighty in a good way. We must believe in their good judgment and their desire for the truth. We must believe that whoever among them made a decision and was right, that this was from Allah Almighty's guidance for

them, and he will get a double reward, and that whoever among them made a decision and was wrong, will only get the reward for his attempt.

2. We are required to check the authenticity of the hadiths circulated amongst us that contain slanderous accusations because after investigating the likes of such hadiths, it will become clear to us that they do not reach the level of weak (*da`if*) or very weak (*da`if jiddan*). Therefore, they should not be relied upon, and no actions should be based on the reprehensible allegations or the corrupt chains of narration contained therein.

Rather, what we surprised to find, and what many are ignorant of, is that such hadiths are invariably fabricated (*mawdoo`ah*) and baseless, and that they were initially made up for the underhanded, vicious, and malicious purposes of:

- Spreading the seed of doubt and denial of the prophethood and messengership of those who were sent amongst those companions who are spoken evil of, since they were his followers, as we explained previously.
- Stirring up dissention and internal conflict among the ranks of the Muslims to weaken them, subdue their strength, and then raise another flag (that of the Jews, Christians, or other innovated beliefs), and we have previously discussed the attempts of Abdullah ibn Saba', the Jew, in that respect.

3. We are required to combine all the authentic hadiths together, for what is hidden to us when we focus only on one particular hadith becomes clear from all the other authentic hadiths between which there is no conflict at all, as long as we examine them closely and try to understand them well in a way that does not contradict the Book of Allah Almighty and the Sunnah of His chosen prophet, Muhammad (sws).

We would now like to summarize what we have presented in the following fashion:

The way the Shia defame the companions of Allah's Messenger (sws) and call them disbelievers, and the way they take this as one of their defining doctrines is, without a shadow of a doubt, corruption in religion and a reprehensible conviction.

Indeed, the insults and accusations which the Shia have invented about the companions of Allah's Messenger (sws) are nothing but reprehensible concoctions and disbelief in the clear noble verses of the Holy Quran, as well as a contradiction of authentic hadiths from Prophet Muhammad (sws).

Many noble verses in the Holy Quran praise the companions of Allah's Messenger (sws) and testify to their virtues. Without a doubt the Perfect, Mighty Book (the Quran), which was sent down by our Lord (Blessed & Most High), with the promise to preserve it, could not contain anything but the truth, and that it will be until the coming of the Hour.

Indeed, Allah (Glorified & Exalted) is the Knower of the Seen and the Unseen. If He (Glorious & Exalted) sent down in His noble verses that which speaks highly of the virtues of the companions of Allah's Messenger (sws) in a Book that will be recited until the coming of the Hour, that can only be due to His Vast, Perfect Knowledge which encompasses everything—everything that was and everything that has not yet been.

Among the noble verses that testify to the virtues of the companions of Prophet Muhammad (sws) and praise them are:

1. The Saying of Allah Almighty,

﴿وَالسَّابِقُونَ الْأَوَّلُونَ مِنَ الْمُهَاجِرِينَ وَالْأَنْصَارِ وَالَّذِينَ اتَّبَعُوهُمْ بِإِحْسَانٍ رَضِيَ اللَّهُ عَنْهُمْ وَرَضُوا عَنْهُ وَأَعَدَّ لَهُمْ جَنَّاتٍ تَجْرِي تَحْتَهَا الْأَنْهَارُ خَالِدِينَ فِيهَا أَبَدًا ذَٰلِكَ الْفَوْزُ الْعَظِيمُ﴾

It means, {**And the first to embrace Islam of the Emigrants and the Helpers and also those who followed them exactly** (in faith). **Allah is well-pleased with them as they are well-pleased with Him. He has prepared for them Gardens under which rivers flow** (Paradise), **to dwell therein forever. That is the supreme success.**}
[Al-Tawbah 9:100]

2. Also, the Saying of Allah Almighty,

﴿لَقَدْ رَضِيَ اللَّهُ عَنِ الْمُؤْمِنِينَ إِذْ يُبَايِعُونَكَ تَحْتَ الشَّجَرَةِ فَعَلِمَ مَا فِي قُلُوبِهِمْ فَأَنْزَلَ السَّكِينَةَ عَلَيْهِمْ وَأَثَابَهُمْ فَتْحًا قَرِيبًا﴾

It means, {**Indeed, Allah was pleased with the believers when they gave their pledge to you under the tree, He knew what was in their hearts, and He sent down tranquility upon them, and He rewarded them with a victory soon to come**}
[Al-Fath 48:18]

Here Allah (Blessed & Exalted) has described the companions of His prophet by praising them, saying that they are people of faith. And that is not all. In fact, He (Glorious & Exalted) brings them the glad tidings of His (Blessed & Most High) Good Pleasure with them.

Undoubtedly, among these noble companions are Abu Bakr al-Siddiq, Umar ibn al-Khattab, and others from the rest of the companions of Allah's Messenger (sws).

3. In addition, there is the Saying of Allah Almighty,

﴿مُحَمَّدٌ رَسُولُ اللَّهِ وَالَّذِينَ مَعَهُ أَشِدَّاءُ عَلَى الْكُفَّارِ رُحَمَاءُ بَيْنَهُمْ تَرَاهُمْ رُكَّعًا سُجَّدًا يَبْتَغُونَ فَضْلًا مِنَ اللَّهِ وَرِضْوَانًا سِيمَاهُمْ فِي وُجُوهِهِمْ مِنْ أَثَرِ السُّجُودِ ذَلِكَ مَثَلُهُمْ فِي التَّوْرَاةِ وَمَثَلُهُمْ فِي الْإِنْجِيلِ كَزَرْعٍ أَخْرَجَ شَطْأَهُ فَآزَرَهُ فَاسْتَغْلَظَ فَاسْتَوَى عَلَى سُوقِهِ يُعْجِبُ الزُّرَّاعَ لِيَغِيظَ بِهِمُ الْكُفَّارَ وَعَدَ اللَّهُ الَّذِينَ آمَنُوا وَعَمِلُوا الصَّالِحَاتِ مِنْهُمْ مَغْفِرَةً وَأَجْرًا عَظِيمًا﴾

{**Muhammad is the Messenger of Allah, and those who are with him are severe against disbelievers, and merciful among themselves. You see them bowing and falling down prostrate** (in prayer), **seeking Bounty from Allah and** (His) **Good Pleasure. The mark of them** (i.e., their faith) **is on their faces** (foreheads) **from the traces of** (their) **prostration** (during prayers). **This is their description in the Torah. But their description in the Gospel is like a** (sown) **seed which sends forth its shoot, then makes it strong, it then becomes thick, and it stands straight on its stem, delighting the sowers—that He may enrage the disbelievers with them. Allah has promised those among them who believe and do righteous good deeds, forgiveness and a mighty reward.**}
[Al-Fath 48: 29]

Here our Lord (Blessed & Exalted) describes the companions of Allah's Messenger (sws) in this noble verse with a multitude of good traits, praising them for sticking by His Messenger (sws) in His Words, ﴿والذين معه﴾ meaning, {**and those who are with him**}, and therefore, assisting and supporting him. He also commends them for being tough against the enemies of Islam in His Words, ﴿أشداء على الكفار﴾ meaning, {**are severe** against disbelievers}. He commends them for being compassionate amongst themselves in His Words, ﴿رحماء بينهم﴾ meaning, {and merciful among themselves}, and He praises them for placing their hope in Him and striving to gain His Good Pleasure in His Words, ﴿يبتغون فضلا من الله ورضوانا﴾ meaning, {seeking Bounty from Allah and (His) Good Pleasure}. Finally, He commends them for their obedience and worship of Him (Glorious & Exalted) in His Words, ﴿سيماهم في وجوههم من أثر السجود﴾ meaning, {The mark of them (i.e., their faith) is on their faces (foreheads) from the traces of (their) prostration (during prayers).}

Besides these there are many verses sent down by Allah (Blessed & Exalted) which praise the companions of His prophet (sws) and testify to their virtues in a Book which will be recited until the Last Day.

This is what the adherents of the Sunnah of the beloved prophet, Muhammad (sws) believe in: we believe in the Book of Allah (Glorious & Exalted) and what He has sent down in the noble verses—praise, commendation, and testament to the virtues of the companions of His prophet, Muhammad (sws). This stands in stark contrast to that which the Shia believe: disbelief in the Book of Allah Almighty (the Holy Quran), insulting and defaming the companions of His prophet (sws) and calling them unbelievers.

Also, many authentic, authoritative hadiths from the Messenger of Allah (sws) have been related which praise his noble companions, commend them, and tell of their virtues. Among them are:

1. His saying (sws),

«لا تسبوا أصحابي، فوالذي نفسي بيده لو أنفق أحدكم مثل أحد ذهبًا ما بلغ مد أحدهم ولا نصيفه»

It means, "Do not insult my companions, for by Him in Whose Hand is my soul, if any of you spent the likes of [Mount] Uhud in gold, it would not value a *mudd* (a specific, small amount) of theirs, nor half."
[Sahih Bukhari]

2. His saying (sws),

«النجوم أمنة للسماء، فإذا ذهبت النجوم أتى السماء ما توعد، وأنا أمنة لأصحابي، فإذا ذهبت أتى أصحابي ما يوعدون، وأصحابي أمنة لأمتي، فإذا ذهب أصحابي أتى أمتي ما يوعدون»

It means, "The stars are the guards of the sky, but when the stars go, what has been promised the sky will befall it. Likewise, I am the guard for my companions, but when I go, what has been promised my companions will befall them. And my companions are the guard of my nation, but when my companions go, what has been promised my nation will befall it."
[Sahih Muslim]

3. His saying (sws),

«إن الله تبارك وتعالى اختارني، واختار لي أصحابًا، فجعل لي منهم وزراءً وأنصارًا وأصهارًا، فمن سبهم فعليه لعنة الله والملائكة والناس أجمعين، لا يقبل منهم يوم القيامة صرفا ولا عدلا»

It means, "**Verily, Allah (Blessed & Exalted) has chosen me and has chosen companions for me, and has made them ministers, supporters, and in-laws for me, so whoever insults them will have the curse of Allah, the Angels, and all people upon him, and, on the Day of Resurrection, no barter or settlement will be accepted.**"

> [Related by al-Haakim, who said its chain of transmission is authentic, and al-Dhahabi agreed]

And there are many other noble prophetic hadiths which praise the companions of Allah's Messenger (sws) and commend him, testifying to their superiority, may Allah Almighty be pleased with them all.

This is what the adherents of the Sunnah of the beloved prophet, Muhammad (sws), are upon: belief in the authentic, authoritative words of Allah's Messenger (sws) which praise, extol, and testify to the virtues of his companions (may Allah be pleased with them all). This stands in stark contrast to what the Shia believe: calling Allah's Messenger (sws) an unbeliever and insulting and slandering his companions (may Allah Almighty be pleased with them) and calling them unbelievers.

Thus, all praise is due to Allah Almighty for the blessing of Islam and for making us among the adherents of the Sunnah of His beloved prophet, Muhammad (sws).

And all praise is due to Allah (Blessed & Exalted) for the gift of guidance and righteousness.

The Shia Belief about Drawing Near to Allah Almighty by Insulting and Cursing Honorable Members of the Prophet's (sws) Household and Why It Is Incorrect

The Shia have invented a reprehensible creed whose existence is rare or perhaps impossible in any of the other false belief systems, namely: insulting, abusing, and cursing, with the belief that such acts will bring them closer to Allah Almighty, to win His Paradise, and be saved from His Fire.

What is even more astounding than that is that this insulting, abusing, and cursing is not directed toward the enemies of Islam and those who seek to destroy it, but rather, it is directed towards the best of all mankind after the prophets and messengers, the best of all those whom history has witnessed their goodly, fragrant stories, the likes of which has not been known in any other epoch (and recorded history bears witness to that fact), to those who supported Prophet Muhammad (sws) since the beginning of his mission, from its emergence to its spread, toward those who raised the flag after him (sws) and reached the ends of the known world, both east and west, north and south, until Allah Almighty took their souls in the best condition (either whilst in remembrance of Allah Almighty or while reciting His Book—Glorious & Exalted—or while fighting for His Cause—Blessed & Most High—or something similar). They direct their venom towards the noble companions whom Allah Almighty chose to accompany His prophet (sws), to assist him, and to support him.

We find no other religion that urges its followers to insult, abuse, and curse their dead (indeed, the best of all the deceased after the prophets and messengers), and to take pleasure in cursing them, except the Shia (and those of their ilk).

It is also strange that those who slander them are those who are of unsound nature and whose rational faculties have not matured. These are the people who make up reprehensible allegations and corrupt doctrines. They do not acknowledge the rights due to the Messenger of Allah (sws), the esteem due to his pure and noble family, or the deference due to his noble companions.

We find those who have not offered this righteous religion anything, but rather were determined to let it be destroyed by its enemies. These are the people who make up such abominable claims and twisted beliefs (seeking Allah Almighty's Favor by insulting and cursing the noble companions of His prophet, sws), and their other false beliefs.

Among the questions that spring to mind which could clarify the reprehensibility of this claim and the corruptness of this belief are those of the following type:

1. Is there not in the insults, abuse, and enjoyment in cursing that the Shia have invented and adopted as creed that which throws morality to the side and would be considered a serious breach of ethics?!!

Answer: Of course, there is.

2. Is there not in the insults, abuse, and cursing that the Shia (and those of their ilk) made up that which would be considered a poor assumption about Allah (Glorious & Exalted), the Supreme Divine Creator and the Wise Legislator?!

Answer: Of course, there is.

3. Would not a chaste and virtuous person feel shy to verbalize such insults, abuse, and cursing against the best of those who believed in the final prophet, Muhammad

(sws), assisted him, and supported him until Allah Almighty took their souls under the best circumstances?!!

Answer: Of course. So, here we have Abu Bakr al-Siddiq, the first caliph to succeed the Messenger of Allah (sws). Allah Almighty took his soul after he fought the apostates after the death of Allah's Messenger (sws), in order to suppress their revolt, while he was engaged in remembrance of Allah (Glorious & Exalted).

Then, there was al-Farouq Umar ibn al-Khattab (the martyr of the prayer niche). Allah Almighty took his soul after the wave of Islamic liberation had spread under his watch and Islam had spread far and wide. He was also engaged in remembrance of Allah Almighty when Abu Lu'lu'ah, the Zoroastrian, proceeded to stab him as he was reciting the Holy Quran while leading the Muslims in prayer.

And there was the 'Possessor of Two Lights,' Uthman ibn `Affan. Allah Almighty made him die a martyr after he had united the Muslims on the Book of Allah Almighty (the Holy Quran), when he collected the Holy Quran into one manuscript. At the time of his martyrdom, he was engaged in reciting the Book of Allah Almighty (the Holy Quran).

To wrap up the questions we have raised:
Why all the insults, abuse, and slander from the Shia towards the best of the Muslims (after the prophets and messengers) from among the followers of the beloved and trustworthy, Muhammad (sws)?!

Why aren't there such insults, abuse, and slander toward non-Muslims, like the Jews, Christians, or others from among the atheists, polytheists, and idol-worshippers (while keeping in mind that the pure Islamic religion does not encourage anything of that sort; it is only meant in accordance with the allegations of the Shia, to show the reprehensibility of their claim)?!!

What does such hatred—like that of the Shia, and those of their ilk, towards the followers and successors of the best of the messengers, Muhammad (sws)—mean?!!

Without a doubt, from what we have brought out in our questions, there is proof of the reprehensibility of the Shia claims, their baseless allegations, and the falseness of their beliefs.

In fact, our questions have brought to light proof of the existence of foreign interventionist plans, manipulation of undisciplined minds, hidden machinations, and plotting against Islam and its true adherents, who uphold its injunctions and the Sunnah of its prophet (sws) and his way, until the Day of Judgment.

The Shia Beliefs about the Imams and the Doctrine of *Bada'* (New Decision), and Why These Are Incorrect

The Shia continued working for a long time to hide the heretical and unorthodox beliefs they harbored from the eyes of the people of *tawhid* (pure Islamic monotheism), the adherents of the Sunnah of the beloved, Muhammad (sws), by acting under a principle known as *taqiyah*. This means that they express outwardly and in their words the opposite of what they believe in their hearts, and what is contained in the major texts which they consider their main sources, they conceal the likes of these statements of disbelief and idolatry.

And so the practice of *taqiyah* continued among the Shia, and those like them, so that they would not be called to account for these idolatrous and blatantly heretical beliefs upon which they base their religion.

However, with the passing of time and the changes in circumstance, what the Shia had long concealed in their hearts came out, and the slanderous allegations and false, corrupt beliefs they harbored became a matter of common knowledge amongst them, among which are:

Believing in the doctrine of the imamate, believing in the 'hidden imam,' and therefore, the invention of the doctrine of *bada'* (new decision) and the denial of Pre-Ordainment!!

To explain:
The Shia claim that they have had twelve imams, or leaders, after Prophet Muhammad's (sws) mission and death, and that the last of these alleged imams was in hiding since childhood and then he went into occultation, completely hidden from the eyes of men, so that no one could see him, and this so-called imam is Muhammad ibn al-Hassan al-`Askari.

Without a doubt, in addition to the reprehensibility of the allegations of the Shia and their doctrine of the imamate, we find a blatant lie in the invention of the imaginary fable concerning the twelfth imam (the last of the alleged imams) because none of the wives or concubines of al-Hassan al-`Askari (who the Shia claim is their twelfth imam) were able to conceive until the moment of his death or afterwards.

According to their beliefs, the Shia claim that their imams are twelve in number and that they are all descended from one another.

As a result, it remains that the twelfth imam does not exist. After the eleventh imam (al-Hassan al-`Askari) proved childless, they invented a story in which he had disappeared since childhood from the eyes of the people until he would reappear at the end of time and come out of occultation, in contempt of reason and bewilderment of the slightest degree of rationality.

Among the details contained in the Shia doctrine of the 'hidden imam'—through which we can see the extent of the disbelief which this renegade sect is mired in—can be seen in the following:

A. The Shia claim that their imam has superpowers, that he knows the unseen, and that the universe is all under his command.

If this is true, then what have they left for Allah Almighty from the Attribute of Divinity, when He (Glorious & Exalted) Alone is deserving of Divinity and Oneness?!!

Nothing strange could be said about this renegade sect when one of their beliefs is also:

B. They believe that Allah Almighty created Muhammad, Ali, and Fatima, then waited for one thousand ages, and then created everything else, so that they witnessed creation, its obedience was bestowed upon them, and its affairs were left to them so that they can permit what they like and prohibit whatever they like. This is what has come in *Usool al-Kaafi*, 1/441 and *Bihaar al-Anwaar*, 25/340.

If this is as the Shia believe, then where is Allah Almighty?!!
And where is His Wisdom and Power (Glorious & Exalted)?!!
And what have they left to Him of the Attributes of Divinity when He (Glorious & Exalted) Alone is deserving of Divinity and Oneness?!!

Also, among the sayings of the Shia which clarify their blatant disbelief through their doctrine of the so-called imams are that:

1. They say that the Lord is the imam who lives on earth.
2. They also say that this world and the Next all belong to the imam; he may do with them as he pleases.
3. Also, the Shia ascribe natural events to the imams.
4. The Shia say that part of the divine light was incarnated in Ali ibn Abi Talib.

And so on, from the blatantly idolatrous and heretical beliefs contained in Shia doctrine (and other sects like them) and recorded in their books.

May Allah (Mighty & Majestic) be exalted over all the fabrications and inventions of the Shia!

How similar the Shia doctrine of the so-called imams is to those who dismantle and disregard the Attributes of the Divine Creator (Glorious & Exalted) until they are rid of Him and they deny His Existence (unbelievers and atheists)!

The Invention of the Doctrine of *Bada'* and the Denial of Pre-Ordainment:
We have already discussed the Shia doctrine of the so-called imams and the claim that their alleged imams know the unseen (the future, remote events, etc.).

These so-called imams used to make predictions, and if one would come true, they would say, "Didn't I tell you that we know the unseen from Allah?" and if reality contradicted what they had said, they would say, "Another matter has occurred (*bada*) to Allah, so He changed what He had informed us of."[7]

As a result, the invention of the Doctrine of *Bada'* (the occurrence of a new decision), which basically says that Allah wants one thing and then it occurs to Him to do the opposite. In other words, what was not apparent to Him becomes apparent, so He changes the information and order to that which has become apparent to Him.[8]

May Allah (Glorious & Most High) be exalted high above all these ridiculous concoctions!

All of this is just an escape from the retribution Allah Almighty visited them with and the scandal He brought upon them in front of those who would make fun of them for the allegations and treacherous, false claims they had made up, so that it would be proof against them on the Day they meet Him (Glorious & Exalted).

Some examples of what the Shia relate from their so-called imams which show the blatant disbelief concealed in their Doctrine of *Bada'* are as follows: the Shia relate from Ja`afar that he used to say that his son, Isma`il, would be the imam after him, but then Isma`il died during his lifetime, so he said, (ما بدا لله في شيء ما بدا في إسماعيل ابني) meaning,

---

[7] *Al-Shia, Shahideen `ala Anfusihim (The Shia, Testifying Against Themsleves)*, by Dr. Diyaa ul-Din al-Kasshif
[8] Ibid.

"Nothing has ever occurred (*bada*) to Allah as it has occurred (*bada*) to Him about my son, Isma`il."

May Allah (Mighty & Majestic) be exalted above the fabrications of the Shia!

In other words, the matter did not stop at openly announcing this corrupt doctrine and the disbelief it contains; rather, he added to it self-conceit and boasting about his son under the cover of this new false claim (the Doctrine of *Bada'*), in contempt of reason, since all of this only increased the so-called imam's followers (who claim him as imam) in obedience and responsiveness. This bears an astonishing resemblance to what Pharoah did with his people when he claimed divinity in contempt of all reason, but they obeyed him and responded to him.

All of this is recorded in the Holy Quran in the Words of the Almighty,

﴿فَاسْتَخَفَّ قَوْمَهُ فَأَطَاعُوهُ﴾

{**Thus he** (Pharoah) **befooled and misled his people, and they obeyed him.**}
[Al-Zukhruf 43: 54]

We seek refuge with Allah Almighty from a corrupted nature and withered reasoning, and may He guide us and bring us back to Him in a beautiful, gentle way.

From this doctrine—the Doctrine of *Bada'*—which the Shia invented, it would be necessary to deny the creed brought by Prophet Muhammad (sws): the obligation to believe in Pre-Ordainment (*al-Qadr*)—that everything that happens in the universe created by Allah Almighty happens with His comprehensive Knowledge (Glorious & Exalted) and with Pre-existing Ordainment in accordance with His Perfect Wisdom (Glorious & Exalted).

Therefore, the Shia have contradicted what the Prophet (sws) came with, and they have defamed the Divine Creator (Glorious & Exalted), negating His Comprehensive Knowledge of everything and the Perfection of His Wisdom....and so on, from the insolence of this corrupt, fabricated doctrine, in conflict with the pure, complete belief of Islamic monotheism (with which Islam came), which recognizes only the worship of Allah (Glorious & Exalted) Alone.

The Shia forgot that Allah (Glorious & Exalted) is not incapable of anything, for He created everything from nothing, and He is the One Who begets not nor was He begotten, and there is none co-equal or comparable unto Him.[9]

From the little we have presented herein, it is abundantly clear that the contents of the Shia doctrine of the alleged imamate—with its idolatry, blatant disbelief, negation of the Oneness of Allah (Glorious & Exalted), and contradiction of the pure and simple focusing of worship on Allah (Glorious & Exalted) which Prophet Muhammad (sws) came with—clearly shows its enormous repugnance and the corruption of its implications, and therefore, its falseness.

And all praise is due to Allah Almighty for the blessing of Islam, and all praise is due to Him for the gift of guidance and righteousness.

---

[9] Please refer to the book, *The Divine Creator: Between the Glorification of the Muslims and the Lies of the Christians and Disbelievers and the Denial of the Atheists*

The Shia Beliefs about Succession and Revelation after the Prophet Muhammad (sws), and Why These Are Incorrect

To begin, let us explain that the Shia made up the idea of the imamate, as we have shown previously in other chapters, and that it was the imam's job to appoint someone to be the imam after him, and that person was supposed to be from his descendants.

Things went on like this (as the Shia claim) until the eleventh alleged imam came, and he was al-Hassan al-`Askari (according to the beliefs of the Shia), but no child was born to him until he died, and none of this wives or concubines got pregnant during his lifetime or after his death.

However, the Shia did not let that stop them. They invented an imaginary son (who didn't really exist) and attributed him to al-Hassan al-`Askari, in order to complete a full twelve, to agree with the number of the tribes of Israel, as taken from the other claims attributed to the so-called Mahdi of the Shia and what he will do when he emerges from hiding underground (according to the beliefs of the Shia).

There is nothing strange in this, since the founder of this renegade sect (the Shia) was the Jew, Ibn Saba', and there is proof of this fact in the books of the Shia themselves. To check, please refer to the book, *Lillah, Thumma lit-Taareekh* (*For Allah, Then for History*), by al-Sayyid Hussain al-Musawi, a Shiite scholar who left the Shia sect and is now following the way of the adherents of the beloved prophet, Muhammad (sws), by the Grace of Allah (Blessed & Most High), and who gives unequivocal textual references from the books of the Shia themselves which confirm that.

Among the proof of the falsehood of this doctrine claimed and contradicted by the Shia are questions raised in the following manner:

1. Isn't prophethood the choice of Allah (Glorious & Exalted) out of Knowledge He (Blessed & Most High) possesses about who should bear the message?

Answer: Of course, it is.

2. As such, is prophethood inheritable? In other words, if death is near to a particular prophet and he has sons, can that prophet pass down the prophethood to one of his sons so that it will not be cut off amongst his descendents?

Answer: Of course not. Prophethood is the choice of Allah Almighty, with full Knowledge and Pre-Ordainment from Him (Glorious & Exalted) of the one who should bear His message so that he will be qualified to do so.

As for what the Holy Quran recorded from the lips of the Prophet of Allah, Zakaria (peace be upon him), in the Almighty's Words,

$$\text{﴿وَإِنِّي خِفْتُ الْمَوَالِيَ مِنْ وَرَائِي وَكَانَتِ امْرَأَتِي عَاقِرًا فَهَبْ لِي مِنْ لَدُنْكَ وَلِيًّا * يَرِثُنِي وَيَرِثُ مِنْ آلِ يَعْقُوبَ وَاجْعَلْهُ رَبِّ رَضِيًّا﴾}$$

It means, {"**And verily! I fear my relatives after me, since my wife is barren. So give me from Yourself an heir, * Who shall inherit** (from) **me, and inherit** (also) **the posterity of Jacob. And make him, my Lord, one with whom You are Well-Pleased!**"}
[Maryam 19: 5-6]

This was merely a wish and a prayer to Allah Almighty and a hope that He (Blessed & Most High) would grant it.

Also, there is the Saying of Allah Almighty, ﴿وَوَرِثَ سُلَيْمَانُ دَاوُدَ﴾ meaning, {**And Solomon inherited** (from) **David**}[Al-Naml 27: 16]

This means: inheritance of the kingdom, and also inheritance of prophethood, with the Full Knowledge and Pre-Ordainment of Allah (Glorious & Exalted), for He (Glorified & Exalted) knows best whom to entrust with the Message. Prophet Solomon's inheritance of prophethood did not mean that is the way it would be from then on, for Prophet Moses (peace be upon him) did not inherit prophethood from anyone, nor did Prophet Jesus (peace be upon him) or Prophet Muhammad (sws).

Prophethood can neither be inherited nor bequeathed at the choice and wish of the individual himself; it is the Choice of Allah (Glorious & Exalted) whom to make a prophet.

If the Shia claim that the imamate is from the religion (falsely and audaciously), and that the imamate is even higher in status than prophethood (erroneously and maliciously), would it be a condition that it be passed down in an unbreakable line from that so-called imam?!!

Answer (in accordance with the fabrications of the Shia): Of course it wouldn't.

Therefore, where does succession come in, let alone the invention of the imamate?! And what does that mean?

Undoubtedly, all of this is meaningless, except to point out the glaring contradiction in Shia doctrine concerning these false allegations and erroneous beliefs.

The Shia have also claimed that the Revelation used to be sent down upon Fatima (may Allah be pleased with her) after the passing of her father (Prophet Muhammad, sws) and that among what was sent down upon her was something called, 'Fatima's Tablet.'

Undoubtedly, such a statement is an erroneous claim, and that is because the Revelation was discontinued from the heavens after the Messages were sealed with the Message of Prophet Muhammad (sws) and his death, and after the Heavenly Scriptures were sealed with the Holy Quran, which was preserved and protected, to guard over all the Books that had previously be sent down.

As a result, there was absolutely no descent for the Guardian of Heavenly Revelation (the Angel Gabriel, peace be upon him) for the purpose of Revelation thereafter.

This is what makes sense to the sound mind, since it is well-known that Allah (Mighty & Majestic) created the angels and made for each one of them a specific job. Among them are those who are entrusted with descent upon the prophets and messengers with the Revelation of Allah Almighty (like Gabriel, peace be upon him) and among them are those who are entrusted with other jobs.

As such, the role of Gabriel (peace be upon him), for which he was designated by Allah Almighty on this earth, was: to bring down Allah Almighty's Revelation from the heavens to the earth, and this is only for Allah Almighty's prophets and messengers who have been selected by Allah (Glorious & Exalted) to invite others to worship Him and to spread His Message.

The question is:
Was Fatima (may Allah be pleased with her) one of the prophets or messengers of Allah Almighty, commanded by Him (Glorious & Exalted) to invite the people to worship Him and spread His Message?!!

Answer: Certainly not.

Prophethood is only for men, not women, as is messengership.

As a result, what conclusions do the lies of the Shia bring us to concerning these false allegations about which we speak?

Without a doubt, this clearly shows the enormous contradiction the Shia encounter, and therefore, the reprehensibility of their claim and the baselessness of their belief.

So, all praise is due to Allah Almighty for the blessing of Islam, and all praise is due to Him for the gift of guidance and righteousness.

The Shia Belief in *Raja'* (Resurrection), a Brief Refutation of this Claim and an Explanation of Why It Is Incorrect

The Shia have made up an astonishingly abominable doctrine which clearly shows the hatred towards Islam and its adherents contained in the souls of those who invented it. The Shia claim that when their twelfth imam reappears, he will bring the Mother of the Believers, Aisha (may Allah be pleased with her), back to life to inflict upon her the death penalty.

Likewise, Abu Bakr and Umar will also be crucified after being raised from the dead. In addition, the twelfth alleged Shia imam will execute all of his political opponents, according to what has come in the Shia books on which they base their deeds, and examples of these books are:

- *Awa'il al-Maqalaat*, by al-Mufid
- *Haqq al-Yaqin*, by Muhammad ibn Baaqir al-Majlisi

In fact, Ibn al-Qimmiy (Babawaih), the leading scholar of Shia hadith, said that most of the Shia sects say that the imams will come back, meaning not just the twelfth imam, but all of them.

Among the questions this raises which would clearly show the error of these Shia claims (and those of their ilk) and therefore the reprehensibility of their allegations and the falseness of their beliefs are the following:

If the Shia belief that the twelfth imam will resurrect Aisha, Abu Bakr, Umar, and other political opponents to execute them and take revenge on them, does that mean that the Shia and those of their ilk have taken the twelfth imam as a god (who gives life, takes it away, and punishes) beside Allah (Glorious & Exalted), or do they claim he shares with Allah Almighty in divinity, or that Allah Almighty granted him part of His Divinity and has given him of His special powers (Glorious & Exalted), or anything else that would lead us to say make up such a vile and egregious thing about Allah Almighty?!!

Did not Allah's Messenger (sws) teach us that this world is the realm of trial, tribulation, and testing, while the Hereafter is the realm of justice?!

Answer: Of course, he did.

Who has the right to contradict the words of the Chosen and Trustworthy, Muhammad (sws), and to make things up to agree with his own desires and to suit his prejudices?

Wasn't Aisha (may Allah be pleased with her) the wife of Prophet Muhammad (sws), and wasn't she from his household? Wasn't she the one who was declared innocent by Allah Almighty from above the seven heavens of the allegations her accusers made against her?!

Answer: Of course, she was.

So why all of this hatred of her? Why all of this animosity and envy towards her?

Also, weren't Abu Bakr and Umar (may Allah be pleased with them) among the first of the noble companions to support Allah's Messenger (sws) and stand by him, fighting in his battles and wars, beginning with the Great Battle of Badr (the first of Prophet

Muhammad's—sws—battles, in which Allah Almighty separated truth from falsehood) until the Battle of Tabuk (the last of Prophet Muhammad's—sws—battles), and then didn't they both walk in the footsteps of their messenger until Allah Almighty took their souls under the best circumstances?!

Answer: Of course.

4. Didn't Allah Almighty reveal verses that lauded them and others among the companions of Allah's Messenger (sws), praising them all?!

Answer: Of course, He did.

Then why all of this hate and envy towards them; indeed, toward the companions (may Allah be pleased with them all)?!!

Undoubtedly questions like these and others lead us to the conclusion that this twisted idea about the Doctrine of Resurrection cannot be the result of anything other than interventionist plotting which found its chance in the midst of sick, withered hearts that then drank their fill of vile beliefs and abominable allegations.
    Hence the determination on the part of the enemies of Allah Almighty and the enemies of His Messenger (sws) that they schemed against Islam from the inside, via those who claim to belong to it, but don't know the first thing about it.
    Thus, anyone who reads these words should not allow himself to be offended by them, if he is sincere, he seeks only the truth, he truly desires it, he walks its path, and he wants salvation in this world and the Next.

As such, we can see the following:
The Doctrine of Resurrection that the Shia (and those of their ilk) invented has absolutely nothing to do with Islam; indeed, it is completely contradictory to what Allah Almighty has informed us in His Wise Book (the Holy Quran) and what His trustworthy prophet, the Seal of Prophets and Messengers, Muhammad (sws), has told us.
    So, all praise is due to Allah Almighty for the blessing of Islam, and all praise is due to Him for the gift of guidance and righteousness.

The Shia Position on Graves, and Therefore, Association of Partners with Allah Almighty

The Shia (and those of their ilk) concurred with what the people of pre-Islamic ignorance were upon before the coming of Prophet Muhammad (sws), in terms of associating partners with Allah (Glorious & Exalted), with the same claims.

The people before Islam claimed that they worshipped idols as a means of drawing near to Him (Glorious & Exalted), and that is how people came to worship others besides Allah (Mighty & Majestic).

Also, we find that the creed of the Shia (and others of their kind) contains the following:

Seeking help from the graves of their so-called imams (and this is blatant association of partners with Allah—Glorious & Exalted—or *shirk*) by claiming that the people in the graves are intercessors between them and Allah (Glorious & Exalted).

(May Allah—Mighty & Majestic—be exalted above having any partners!)

The Shia made the graves of their imams into idols worshipped beside Allah (Glorious & Exalted).

The Shia made visiting graves and tombs among the obligations of its school of law, even pilgrimage to them and circumambulation of them, formal and informal prayer before them, plus kissing their thresholds, and more of these heretical, idolatrous rites.[10]

We seek refuge with Allah Almighty from associating anything with Him, when He has guided us and brought us back to Him in a gentle, beautiful way.

Allah (Mighty & Majestic) has said in His Perfect Book (the Holy Quran),

﴿إِنَّ اللَّهَ لَا يَغْفِرُ أَنْ يُشْرَكَ بِهِ وَيَغْفِرُ مَا دُونَ ذَلِكَ لِمَنْ يَشَاءُ وَمَنْ يُشْرِكْ بِاللَّهِ فَقَدِ افْتَرَى إِثْمًا عَظِيمًا﴾

It means, {**Verily, Allah forgives not that partners should be set up with Him in worship, but He forgives except that to whom He pleases, and whoever sets up partners with Allah in worship has indeed invented a tremendous sin.**}
[Al-Nisaa' 4: 48]

Among that which can corroborate the corruptness of the beliefs we have shown the Shia (and those of their ilk) to base their religion on is what the Shiite scholar, al-Majlisi, has mentioned in *Bihaar al-Anwaar*, when he said, "Facing the graves is a necessary thing, even if it is not in the same direction as the *qiblah* (the direction of the Kaäba in Mecca)."

In fact, other Shia scholars prefer the worshipper to face the grave and turn his back to the Kaäba during the prayer for visiting (the grave).

The Shaikh of the Shia (al-Musawi and al-Tousi) have written a book in which they make pilgrimage to the graves like pilgrimage to the Kaäba.

Among other scholars of the Shia (and those of their ilk), there are those who make pilgrimage to the graves greater than pilgrimage to the Kaäba.

And the Shia (and those of their ilk) have still more heretical, idolatrous sayings, but to bring this point to a close, we would like to raise some important questions in the following manner:

Can anyone of pure human nature, as it was created by Allah Almighty to worship only Him, accept the likes of these corrupt beliefs and what they contain of idolatry and blatant disbelief?!

---

[10] *Al-Shia, Shahideen `ala Anfusihim* (with minor editing), by Dr. Diyaa' ul-Din al-Kaashif

Answer: Certainly not.

Can anyone of sound, righteous mind, as granted him by Allah Almighty to be used properly and employed for deep thinking about His Signs (Glorious & Exalted), and therefore, to confess His Divinity and Oneness tolerate this blatant idol-worship and open heresy?!!

Answer: Certainly not.

Is what the Shia (and those of their ilk) take as their religion the Islam that the Seal of the Prophets and the Head of the Messengers, the beloved and trustworthy, Muhammad (sws), came with?!!

Answer: Most certainly not.

Prophet Muhammad (sws) came with *tawhid*: pure, unadulterated monotheism which singles out worship for Allah (Glorified & Exalted) Alone.

Is what the Shia (and those of their ilk) take as their religion the pure Islamic monotheism which the trustworthy prophet, Muhammad (sws), continued to invite the people to?!!

Answer: It most certainly is not.

Therefore, what is it that the Shia (and those like them) take as their religion? And what does that prove?

Undoubtedly, the likes of that which the Shia take as their religion and believe in is nothing other than the opposite of *tawhid*; it is idol-worship and blatant disbelief. It conforms with the religion of Pre-Islamic Ignorance, and also with the error and misguidance of the extreme Sufis.

All of this proves how far the Shia have strayed from Allah's Straight Path and the Righteous Way of His prophet (sws), due to the evil plans hatched at the outset of this renegade sect at the hand of Ibn Saba', the Jew, who demeaned the intellect of his followers, who responded to the corruption of his speech and the abominable nature of his call, to scheme against Islam and its adherents.

So all praise is due to Allah Almighty for the blessing of Islam, and all praise is due to Him for the gift of guidance and righteousness.

The Shia's Glorification of Those in the Graves, Seeking Help from Them, and Taking Them as Intercessors with Allah Almighty

To start, we would like to clarify that Allah (Glorified & Exalted) is the Supreme Divine Creator, and as a result, He (Glorious & Exalted) is the One Who Alone deserves to be worshipped and Who Alone can be singled out with Greatness.

The *Tawhid*, or the Oneness, of Allah Almighty, becomes clear in relation to us and our worship of Him (Glorified & Exalted) Alone—our seeking refuge and support with Him and our seeking help and succor with Him (Glorious & Exalted) Alone—and therefore, He Alone deserves the description of pure Greatness and Glory.

However, in the case of seeking refuge and support with people in graves and seeking help and succor from them as in the doctrine of the Shia, purporting to take them as a means of getting closer to Allah Almighty, this entails the association of partners with Allah (Glorious & Exalted), which is the negation of *tawhid*. It means the association of a created being with the Greatness and Glory which must be singled out for Him (Glorified & Exalted) Alone.

And Allah (Mighty & Majestic) cannot allow anyone to share with Him in His Oneness or anything to compete with His Greatness.

The polytheists of Mecca before the coming of Prophet Muhammad (sws) used to take idols and worship them and seek help from them. They used to say that they were content to worship them as a means of drawing near to Allah Almighty, but this worship did not benefit them in the least; rather, it is what turned them into disbelievers, deserving of Allah Almighty's Wrath and an eternity of His Punishment.

Contrary to all of this, we find that the adherents of the Sunnah of our beloved prophet, Muhammad (sws), are the ones who remained steadfast on what Prophet Muhammad (sws) came with, in terms of pure, sound beliefs, based only upon *tawhid*, the worship of Allah (Glorious & Exalted) Alone, not associating anything or anyone in worship with Him, and based upon singling Him (Glorious & Exalted) out for Perfect Greatness without letting anything compete with Him.

Thus there is but one truth, and it is the light with which Allah Almighty erases the darknesses.

The Shia and Their (Illegitimate) Seeking of Blessing, Plus Their Belief that Others Besides Allah Can Benefit Them

The Shia (and those of their ilk) have gone to extremes in their understanding of *tabarruk*, seeking blessing. In other words, their definition of *tabarruk* is: the belief that benefit can be derived from the thing blessing is being sought from. And this is *shirk*: association of partners with Allah (Glorious & Exalted).

Benefit and harm are only in the Hand of Allah (Glorious & Exalted) Alone, not in any of His creations.

If the Arabs before the coming of Islam (bringing them out of the darkness of *shirk* and the worship of idols to the light of *tawhid* and the worship of Allah Almighty, the One, the Judge) used to seek blessing from idols and stones, today we find the Shia (and those of their kind) rejecting the principles of Islam, taking a path other than that with which Prophet Muhammad (sws) came. They have raised the banner of idolatry once more and returned to what was before Islam. We find them seeking blessing from the clay from which the grave of one of the men they regard as holy (al-Hussain) was made and believing that it can benefit them without Allah Almighty (that is, if the grave is actually the resting place of al-Hussain, for there are many countries that all claim al-Hussain was buried there).

In fact, you find them prostrating to the ground on a certain kind of clay obtained from a certain place. The Shiite carries a disc made of this particular material, and he believes it benefits him and blesses him when he places his forehead on it each time he prays.

May Allah (Mighty & Majestic) be exalted above the association of partners with Him!

Untainted human nature, pure souls, and righteous, sound minds reject the association of partners with Allah Almighty or any competition for His Oneness and Greatness.

Prophet Muhammad (sws) was sent by Allah (Blessed & Most High) with the message of pure *tawhid*: to worship none but Allah (Glorious & Exalted), and as a result, for close to thirteen long years after he was sent as a prophet to Mecca, Prophet Muhammad (sws) used to invite the people to worship only Allah Almighty and to renounce association of partners and idol-worship, and he used to work to train his companions well in this respect.

The legislative aspects of the religion were only sent down after his (sws) migration to Medina. They were revealed to pure, clean, and righteous hearts that were singularly devoted in worship and which glorified the Greatness of Allah (Glorious & Exalted).

As a result, the noble companions, who were trained by Prophet Muhammad (sws) for thirteen long years to worship only Allah (Glorious & Exalted), were the ones who assisted and supported him until his call was successful and until his Message was announced openly and spread.

In fact, the companions (may Allah Almighty be pleased with them) are the ones who took up the banner of this religion (Islam) after him (sws) and brought it to the ends of the known world, east and west, north and south, traveling in his wake, following in his path, and walking in his footsteps. As such, it was Allah (Mighty & Majestic) who granted them this success, aided them, supported them, and honored the religion through them. So, may Allah Almighty be pleased with them all until the Last Day.

Also, we find that the companions of Prophet Muhammad (sws) were molded in this pure monotheism to worship only Allah (Glorious & Exalted) since the advent of Islam, and they were the quickest to apply the laws revealed by Allah (Mighty & Majestic), out of obedience and devotion to it, but this was not until after their hearts had been purified from the filth of idolatry and the belief that others besides Allah (Glorious & Exalted) could benefit them.

The companions of Prophet Muhammad (sws) would not have experienced this support and steadfastness from Allah (Mighty & Majestic) for them if their hearts had contained hypocrisy or idolatry of the likes of that which we find the ranks of Shia societies doing today, and indeed, that which even their scholars and learned men actually encourage.

So, all praise is due to Allah (Blessed & Most High) for keeping this true, unadulterated religion of Islam in check through the righteous scholars from the adherents of the Sunnah of our beloved prophet, Muhammad (sws), preserving its directives and holding fast to His book (the Holy Quran) and the Sunnah of His prophet, Muhammad (sws), inviting others to it, and spending everything valuable and precious to bring it victory.

All praise is due to Allah (Blessed & Most High) for making us Muslims, from the adherents of the Sunnah of the beloved and trustworthy prophet, Muhammad (sws).

Practical Examples of the Heretical Beliefs of the Shia

Practical examples of *shirk*, or idolatry, in the Shia creed (and those like them) are plentiful, so perhaps on this point it would be enough to mention just one example in brief, just for clarity.

The Shia (and those of their ilk) have made seeking help at the graves of their so-called imams a requirement for the fulfillment of their issues and needs.

(May Allah Almighty protect us from this blatant sin and guide us to His Straight Path!)

Examples of this are:
The Shia (and those of their ilk) say that if you have a need for Allah (Mighty & Majestic), write a prayer and throw it upon the grave of one of the imams.[11]

In other words, if there is something a person wishes he could have, like success on an exam or to have a child, etc., he should write what he wants or needs on a piece of paper and then put it on the grave of any of the so-called Shia imams since they believe that the person in the grave on which the piece of paper is placed will give him what he wants, that he will carry out the wish that was written on the paper as long as it was that person who wanted it and not someone else.

Among the important questions that come to mind here is: Where is Allah (Glorious in His Majesty)???

Where are faith and the belief in the Divine Creator (Glorious & Exalted)?!!

Where is the worship of none but Allah (Glorious & Exalted)???

What have the Shia (and those of their ilk) left for Allah (Glorious & Exalted) of the Attributes of Divinity?? Where are the hearts with awareness and insight?? Where are the minds that understand and comprehend??

Can pure human nature, purified souls, and righteous minds accept the likes of these corrupt beliefs (which the Shia and those of their ilk take as their religion) and the obvious idolatry and blatant disbelief contained therein??

Certainly not.

Prophet Muhammad (sws) came with Islam to bring the people out of the darkness and into the light, out of *shirk* and into *tawhid*, from the worship of idols to the worship of the Lord of the worshippers (Allah—Glorious & Exalted).

So, all praise is due to Allah Almighty for the blessing of Islam, and all praise is due to Allah Almighty for the gift of guidance and righteousness.

---

[11] *Al-Shia, Shahideen `alaa Anfusihim (The Shia, Testifying Against Themselves)*, by Dr. Diyaa' ul-Din al-Kaashif

Religious Rituals of the Shia

One of the most prominent marks of the Shia is that during their religious celebrations, we find them bashing their heads and flogging themselves with chains and knives, as can be seen at the celebrations on the Day of Ashoura.

Perhaps the reader will be shocked at the likes of such behavior, asking himself:

1. Is what I am reading the truth or is it some kind of exaggeration?
2. Does this really happen?
3. What kind of religion would order such outrageous folly?
4. Did the Seal of the Prophets and Messengers, Muhammad (sws), come with the true, unadulterated Islamic religion and its liberal legislation in order to command the likes of such nonsense which would keep people from entering Islam, or even make its adherents a joke for all nations, east to west?!

And the answer to the likes of such a question (over which there can be no dispute) is:

What we have mentioned is absolute fact. If the reader is struck by surprise at what we have mentioned, he may observe these festivals with his own eyes, especially in the age of satellite television and the Internet. Then he will not only be struck by surprise; he will be horrified by what he sees—the sight of the blood among man and women, and even among the young and children.

As such, the reader may, with minimal effort, check that what we have mentioned does actually occur, for real, through the Internet.

The answer to the third question is:

No religion on the face of the earth would order such outrageous folly; it is but a whim which, if not controlled by the limits of Allah's Laws (Glorious & Exalted), would cause people to act senselessly and haphazardly, leading him away from Allah's Straight Path.

The answer to the fourth question is:

The true, unadulterated religion of Islam and its liberal legislation bears no responsibility for the ridiculous acts the Shia have taken as their religion.

Prophet Muhammad (sws) did not come with this righteous religion and its noble rightly-guiding rites of worship which conform to untainted human nature, are in harmony with pure souls, and which are acceptable to sound, righteous minds. This is what the adherents of the Sunnah of our beloved prophet, Muhammad (sws), hold fast to and invite the people to.

As a result, we see many, many people entering Allah's religion (Islam) in droves, from the east of the globe to the west.

Thus, all praise is due to Allah Almighty for the blessing of Islam, and all praise is due to Allah Almighty for the gift of guidance and righteousness.

The Doctrine of the Clay in Which the Shia Believe, a Brief Refutation of It and an Explanation of Why It Is Incorrect

We would like to briefly explain the Doctrine of the Clay in which the Shia (and those of their ilk) believe, in two respects:

The first issue:
By clay, the Shia mean the soil of the grave of al-Hussain. They claim that from it comes healing, and therefore, blessing may be sought from it.

Without a doubt, this doctrine alleged by the Shia is *shirk*, or association of partners with Allah (Glorious & Exalted) since the Shia (and those of their kind) believe that benefit and blessing comes from this clay, without Allah Almighty, because al-Hussain ibn Ali was buried there. In more precise terms:

The Shia believe that the benefit is in al-Hussain ibn Ali. Indeed, the Shia scholars (and those like them) are the ones who call the people to the likes of such disbelief, idolatry, and more.

As such, this claim is a horrendous allegation and a false doctrine.

And Allah (Glorified & Exalted) is the Most Self-Sufficient, and He does not need partners, nor does He accept them.

The second issue:
The Shia (and those of their kind) claim that the Shiite was created from a special kind of clay, and the Sunni (the adherent of the Sunnah of our beloved prophet, Muhammad, sws) was created from another kind of clay, and as such, the sins and crimes committed by a Shiite are a result of him being affected by the clay from which the Sunni was created, and the goodness and trustworthiness of a Sunni is the result of him being affected by the clay from which the Shiite was created. Then, when the Day of Resurrection comes, the major and minor sins of the Shia will be put on the Sunnis and the good deeds of the Sunnis will be put on the Shia.[12]

Before raising some questions to show the fallaciousness and reprehensibility of this doctrine, we would like to raise certain questions to demonstrate the interventionist, foreign source of these ideas and beliefs that the Shia hold. It was a plot against Islam by way of some of those who claim to belong to it, but who do not know anything about it. This can be seen in the following way:

Why do the Shia single out the adherents of the Sunnah of Prophet Muhammad (sws) for all this enmity?!!

Where is the clay from which the Jew, the Christian, and those of other false creeds that deny the prophets and messengers of Allah Almighty were created?!!

Indeed, where is the clay from which the atheists were made when they do not even confess the Existence of the Divine Creator (Glorious & Exalted)?!! Is there a special type of clay from which they were created?!! Or is the issue limited to the adherents of the Sunnah of our beloved prophet, Muhammad (sws)?!!

And so on.

Undoubtedly, all of this proves that the seed of hatred in the hearts of the Shia (through their false doctrines) towards the adherents of the Sunnah of our beloved prophet, Muhammad (sws), was planned. It was a clever plot, a strategy of the enemies

---

[12] `Aqaa'id al-Shi`ah (*The Shia Creed*—with minor editing—by Abdullah Muhammad al-Salafi, taken from: `Ilal al-Sharaai` and *Bihaar al-Anwaar* (among the books of the Shia)

of Islam to get at it and at those who hold fast to the example and Sunnah of he who came to proclaim it—our beloved prophet, Muhammad (sws).

Here we must raise still more questions in order to demonstrate the falseness of the doctrines of the Shia (and those of their ilk), the reprehensibility of their call, and the enormity of their lies and defamation, which we will do in the following manner:

Isn't Allah Almighty the Divine Creator, Who does not injustice the weight of an atom or even less than that?!

Answer: Of course He is. Allah Almighty is the True God, Who has forbidden injustice and oppression for Himself and made it prohibited among the people.

Can what the Shia (and those of their kind) claim—that the adherents of the Sunnah of our beloved prophet, Muhammad (sws), will carry the sins and transgressions of the Shia (according to their alleged Doctrine of the Clay)—be considered Allah Almighty's Justice which permits no injustice or oppression of the people at all?!!

Answer: Certainly not.

Isn't what the Shia claim and take as doctrine pure fabrication and audacity before Allah Almighty?!!

Answer: Of course, it is.

Aren't all people equal before Allah Almighty, with no superiority of Arab over non-Arab, nor non-Arab over Arab, except in terms of fear of Allah (Glorious & Exalted) and righteous good deeds, just as the Trustworthy, Prophet Muhammad (sws) taught us?!

Answer: Of course, they are.

Shouldn't this allegation, taken by the Shia as doctrine, be considered a poor assumption about Allah (Glorious & Exalted), and a diminishment and devaluation of His Attributes?!!

Answer: Of course, it should.

Didn't Allah (Glorified & Exalted) tell us in His Perfect Book (the Holy Quran), in His Words (Glorious & Exalted): ﴿أَلَّا تَزِرُ وَازِرَةٌ وِزْرَ أُخْرَى﴾ meaning, {**That no burdened person** (with sins) **shall bear the burden** (sins) **of another**}[Al-Najm 53: 38] In other words, no one will have to bear the sins and transgressions of another, or no person will be responsible for another's sins or the cause of another's misguidance?!!

Answer: Of course, He did.

So what does it prove that the Shia contradict the Words of their Lord (Glorious & Exalted) and go against the injunctions of their prophet (sws)?!!

And what if one of the Shia were to turn back to Allah's Straight Path, walk in the footsteps of His righteous prophet (sws), and imitate his example, following the people of his Sunnah (sws)?!!

From what clay would the Shia claim he had been created?!!

Was he from the clay of the Shia or the clay of the adherents of the Sunnah of Prophet Muhammad (sws)?!!
And so on.

From the little we have said, there is clear proof of the enormity of the insolence and lies of the Shia about Allah Almighty, and therefore, the abomination of their call and their twisted doctrines.

So, all praise is due to Allah Almighty for the blessing of Islam, and all praise is due to Him for the gift of guidance and righteousness.

The Shia Belief about Karbala
and Why It Is Incorrect

The Shia (and those of their ilk) have claimed that the graves of their so-called imams are sacred sites. They have also claimed that Karbala is superior to the Holy Kaäba in Mecca.

Our question on this point is as follows:

Wasn't the Holy Kabah chosen by Allah Almighty to be the first house placed on the earth to worship Him Alone, to establish *tawhid*, and to get rid of any partners associated with Him?!!

Answer: Of course, it was.

Would it be possible after that to imagine that any other place could be equal to Mecca?!!

Answer: Certainly not.

Wasn't the Holy City of Mecca chosen by Allah (Blessed & Most High) to be the cradle of His worldwide message and the seal of all previous messages?!

Answer: Of course, it was.

So what does that prove??

Without a doubt, this clearly proves the great sacredness of this blessed and holy place, and that Mecca is the most beloved city to Allah Almighty, and therefore, to His Messenger, Muhammad (sws)—as he (sws) told us—and that no other location could equal its status.

Wasn't the Holy Kaäba chosen by Allah Almighty as the *qibla*, or direction of prayer, for the Muslims, which He sanctioned for them after Allah's Messenger (sws) had long been yearning to pray towards it before the *qibla* was changed from the direction of Jerusalem?!!

Answer: Of course, it was.

Aren't the Holy Cities of Mecca and Medina the only ones that will be protected by Allah (Blessed & Most High) from being entered by the Antichrist, and therefore, from his evil at the Endtimes, as we were informed by Prophet Muhammad (sws)?!!

Answer: Of course, they are.

So what does that prove??

Without a doubt, this proves what has been made clear in the answers to the preceding questions: that no other place on earth can equal the Holy City of Mecca in sacredness and status before Allah (Glorified & Exalted).

It also proves that whoever contradicts reason and goes against the words of the Messenger (sws) (who informed us that Mecca was the most beloved city to Allah Almighty and to him, sws), and who even comes saying something so far removed from that which sound minds could accept and from that which has been established in the authentic, authoritative source texts, such as claiming sacred status for the city of

Karbala and that it is superior to Mecca, even though it is just a city like any other city, and there is not a single hadith from Prophet Muhammad (sws) about its superiority or sacredness (except for those invented by the Shia through pure lies and fabrication), then this confirms the enormity of the affront to Allah Almighty and the impugnation of His Messenger (sws), and therefore, the reprehensibility of this call and the fallaciousness of this belief.

So, all praise is due to Allah Almighty for the blessing of Islam, and that He made us among the followers of the Sunnah of the best of the messengers, our beloved and trustworthy prophet, Muhammad (sws).

And all praise is due to Allah Almighty for the gift of guidance and righteousness.

The Shia Belief about the Mahdi

The Mahdi, according to the Shia claim, is Ibn al-Hassan al-Askari.

First of all, what the Shia claim is a pure lie. That is because al-Hassan al-Askari, who the Shia claim is their eleventh imam, did not have a son; none of his wives or concubines ever got pregnant, either before or after his death.

The proof of this is also that:

None of the Shia themselves ever saw this alleged son, who was falsely and astonishingly invented and made an imam.

Indeed, it was to avoid the lie and their true reality from being discovered that the Shia claimed that this Mahdi had two hidden forms: one little, whom no one had ever seen except those who were close to him, and another big, such that he went into hiding underground and disappeared from the eyes of all, including the scholars and learned men of the Shia.

Undoubtedly, all of this was pure lies, unacceptable and unbelievable to anyone of sound mind, which demonstrates that the Shia claim of the imamate is false to the core.

The untenable reason for the Shia claim that the Mahdi is in hiding and has been in occultation for over one thousand years:

The Shia claim that their twelfth imam, Muhammad ibn al-Hassan al-Askari (who we previously noted is a character falsely and outrageously invented because al-Hassan al-Askari did not have any son to become imam), who is known as *Saahib al-Zamaan,* or the Owner of Time, went into hiding when he was five years old because he was afraid he would be killed. The Shia compare that to when Allah's Messenger (sws) went into hiding in the cave during his escape and migration from Mecca to Medina.

Without a doubt, this is a departure from reason, and it bewilders the requirements of logic because that analogy on which an entire creed was built is completely absurd. It is like someone saying, "Your excuse is uglier than your offense," since the differences between the two are so wide. Among them are:

1. Prophet Muhammad (sws) did not hide from the sight of the world; his mission in the beginning was secret until it began to bear good fruit, but it was not long before he was commanded by Allah Almighty to proclaim his Message openly, especially in the place he and his companions had been persecuted in Mecca.

    After Allah Almighty ordered His prophet (sws) to migrate from Mecca to Medina, he took all the necessary steps to travel, placing his trust in Allah Almighty. One of these steps was that, when he found out that the Meccans were looking for him while he was on his way out, he and his friend, Abu Bakr al-Siddiq (may Allah be pleased with him), hid in a cave, but it was only for three nights, not for over one thousand years (as the Shia claim about their alleged Mahdi). Then he (sws) and his friend continued their migration to Medina to fulfill his mission and proclaim the Message.[13]

2. During his migration, Prophet Muhammad (sws) was accompanied by his friend, Abu Bakr al-Siddiq (may Allah be pleased with him), and other people aided him in his journey as well.[14]

    As for the Mahdi claimed by the Shia (their twelfth imam), no one saw him because in reality, he didn't exist, as we have shown previously.[15]

---

[13] *Rabihtu al-Sahabah wa Lam Akhsar Aal al-Bait (I Gained the Companions and I Didn't Lose the Prophet's Family)*—with minor editing—by Abu Khalifah ibn Ali Muhammad al-Qadiyy

[14] Ibid.

3. Prophet Muhammad (sws) hid so that he could reemerge, since he was coming back to continue inviting people to Islam, and therefore, he came to have followers to help him, back him, and assist him in his call. The Shia Mahdi, on the other hand, did not have a mission in the first place, and therefore, he does not have any followers, which is why the Shia invented the idea of his hiding and occlusion underground.[16]

From the little we have shown here, the untenable reasoning of the Shia should be clear, for it is an insult to human intelligence. It is an affront to the faculty of reasoning given to us by Allah Almighty to distinguish good from bad, the fine from the poor, and the robust from the feeble.

Of all the comments which would clarify the fallaciousness of the doctrine of the Shia concerning the twelfth imam—who await his reemergence from occultation—and show its contradiction to sound reasoning, we present the following:

Why doesn't the Shia Mahdi appear on the television screens when we now live in the age of satellite television and the Internet, or at least, on videotape as do many revolutionary political figures (who fear their opponents and are fighting the powers that be), and give it to people who claim from time to time to be in contact with them (in other words, without delivering it himself) if he so fears his enemies and opponents?

From this imaginary scenario invented by the Shia about their Mahdi, others moved into action to get a piece of the enormous fortune represented in the war booty and what his underground hiding place gets in donations which are collected based on the claim that they are part of the preparations for the emergence of the Mahdi after a long time spent in hiding, so they claimed that they are the Mahdi's representatives who must take possession of this vast fortune.

The strange thing, which goes against untainted human nature, purified souls, and sound, righteous minds, is that we find the scholars from Shia territory encouraging the spread of all kinds of corruption and all types of oppression, by claiming that this accelerates the emergence of this so-called Mahdi.

Undoubtedly, this is not the religious law with which the true, unadulterated Islamic religion came. It is not the injunctions of Prophet Muhammad (sws); rather, it is misguidance, leading people away from the religion of Allah (Mighty & Majestic)—Islam, if it were to be understood in the way of the Shia (and those of their ilk).

Allah Almighty is the Truth, and He does not ever condone corruption and oppression.

Testament to that fact is what Allah Almighty ordered us in terms of the reformation and negation of corruption on the earth and the establishment of justice between Muslims and non-Muslims, whether they are among those who disbelieve in Him (Glorious & Exalted) or deny the prophethood of any of His prophets or messengers.

What the Shia Mahdi will supposedly do, with refutation:
In reality, what the Shia claim their twelfth imam, known as al-Qa'im, or the Awaited Mahdi, will do to see to it that the heedless will awake from his oblivion and the reasonable person will use his mind to seek out Allah's Straight Path, is what no person of unspoiled human nature, purified soul or sound mind could remain neutral about.

Here are some examples of the things that will purportedly be done by the Mahdi whose emergence from hiding the Shia await and whose veracity they allege, and therefore, who they believe in:

---

[15] Ibid.
[16] *Rabihtu al-Sahabah wa Lam Akhsar Aal al-Bait (I Gained the Companions and I Didn't Lose the Prophet's Family)*—with minor editing—by Abu Khalifah ibn Ali Muhammad al-Qadiyy.

1. The Shia claim that their twelfth imam, when he emerges from hiding, will take the sword to the Arabs and kill them.

Among the questions which will show the fallaciousness of this vile belief and which proves the reprehensibility of the Shia message (and those of their ilk) and that many dirty hands have manipulated them and their minds since the initial establishment of this sect at the hands of its founders, we present the following:

- Wasn't Muhammad (sws)—the final prophet who sealed all previous divine messages—an Arab?!
- Weren't the noble companions—those who believed in him, his call, and his Message, who aided and supported him—Arabs?!
- Weren't the noble companions (may Allah Almighty be pleased with them all) and their followers—those who bore the concerns of this religion and raised its mighty banner until it brought them to the ends of the known world, east and west—Arabs?!
- Wasn't the family of Prophet Muhammad (sws) also Arabs?!
- Isn't the Mahdi an Arab?!
- and so on...

Don't these questions lead us to believe that Allah Almighty chose the Arabs over all others to bring out from them those who would lead the world to His Straight Path?!

And therefore, why all this hatred towards the Arabs?!!

The answer to these questions emerges when the truth which remains hidden to many people appears, and that is:

The lands of Persia, which now largely resembles the country of Iran, have not forgotten that the Arabs are the ones who deposed Chosroes (the King of Persia) from his throne after he completely refused to accept Islam during the Islamic conquest and liberation and their invitation to worship Allah Alone. Hence this epic hatred from the lands of Persia (those of them who do not believe, that is) towards the Arabs, and it is this resentment which was used by dirty hands to manipulate unaware minds into coming up with a treacherous creed to battle the people of Islam and the adherents of the Sunnah of our beloved prophet, Muhammad (sws), thereby.

And why is this long-lost fact so shocking when it is well-known that the Shia, whose main homeland is Iran, claim that Chosroes (the heretic, who chose not to believe) was saved by Allah from the Hellfire?! Who in their right mind would accept the likes of such manipulation of words?!

Indeed, the Shia have given Abu Lu'lu'ah al-Majusi (the disbeliever who killed Umar ibn al-Khattab) the name, Baba Shujaa`al-Din, or the Courage of the Religion, and they began to celebrate at his grave and built a large structure over it for the festivities.

May Allah Almighty preserve us from corruption of the mind, from arrogance, and from giving into our own whims and grudges!

2. Another claim the Shia make about the emergence of their twelfth imam is that he will bring Abu Bakr al-Siddiq and al-Farooq Umar (may Allah be pleased with them) back to life to crucify them. They also say the same thing about Aisha (may Allah be pleased with her), the Mother of the Believers—that they will bring her back to like to stone her to death, and so on.

Among the questions that would demonstrate the corruption of this belief the Shia hold and the vileness of their call, and which would uncover the veiled hatred in the hearts of its adherents which leads them to such fables and legends, are the following:

- Does anyone beside Allah (Glorious & Exalted) possess the power to bring the dead back to life for judgment and punishment or do the Shia claim divinity for their awaited imam?!
- If the Shia respond that their so-called imam's ability to bring the dead to life is but a power granted to him from Allah Almighty, isn't the judgment and punishment he meets out to them a form of insubordination before Allah Almighty and a competition with Him in the Attributes of Divinity, since reward and punishment are in His (Glorious & Exalted) Hand Alone?!
- Or do the Shia claim that Allah Almighty has deputized their so-called imam and permitted him to share in His Divinity?!
- Isn't this world the realm of trials and tribulations from Allah Almighty and isn't the Hereafter the realm of reward and punishment? Or have the Shia abolished that for the same motive as that which pits them against the noble companions of Prophet Muhammad (sws) and the pure prophetic household: malice anchored in the souls of its adherents at the hands of agents provocateurs who worked to sow the seeds of this sect and to make it grow?!
- Why do the Shia claim that their imam will take revenge on the noble companions and the pure prophetic household while leaving the Jews, Christians and others from among the atheists, polytheists and pagans?!

Don't such questions lead us to conclude that the corrupt beliefs the Shia hold and their repugnantly contradictory claims are nothing but the result of a pre-planned strategy to get at Islam and its adherents by carrying away its members: the followers of the Sunnah of our beloved prophet, Muhammad (sws).

3. Among the Shia claims about the emergence of their twelfth imam (al-Qa'im or al-Mahdi) is that he will destroy the Holy Mosque in Mecca and the Prophet's Mosque in Medina and that he will change the *qibla*, or direction of prayer, to the city of Kufa (in Iraq), after bringing the Black Stone (currently built into the corner of the Kaäba) there from Mecca.

Among the questions which would show the fallaciousness of this vile belief, and therefore, the abominable Shia message, and reveal the twisted plans at work under the cover of this renegade sect, established at the hand of Ibn Saba', the Jew, are the following:

- How could the Holy Mosque in Mecca be destroyed when it is the first house built solely for the worship of Allah (Mighty & Majestic) on the earth we live on, with His Knowledge and Selection (Glorious & Exalted)?!
- How can the Holy Mosque in Mecca be destroyed when it is the *qibla* that Allah's Messenger (sws) so frequently used to yearn to pray toward (before the direction of prayer was switched from Jerusalem to Mecca)?!
- How could the Holy Mosque in Mecca and the Prophet's Mosque in Medina be destroyed when the Seal of the Prophets and Messengers, Muhammad (sws), prayed in them; indeed, he longed to pray in them due to the enormity of the reward from Allah (Blessed & Most High)?!

Is this what the Shia are waiting for their Mahdi to do: killing Muslims and the people of Islam and demolishing its landmarks, after hiding for over one thousand years?!

If that is what the Shia (and their so-called imam) are waiting for, then how similar are they to the Jews waiting for their false Messiah who will also come to wreak havoc on the earth and spread lies and injustice.!!

Indeed, what the Shia claim about the hidden imam they are waiting for is unequivocal proof for all those of untainted human nature and sound minds of the abominable message of the Shia, and therefore, the fallacious nature of their beliefs, and this is after wicked hands have manipulated the minds of their people.

4. Among the claims of the Shia about when their twelfth imam will emerge is that he will implement the law of the line of David/Dawud and brush the Quran aside, and no proof will be asked.

Among the questions that would show the falseness of this corrupt belief and prove the reprehensible message of the Shia, and therefore, shed light on the secret relationship between the Shia and the Jews, after they administered their poison to them (in their beliefs), are:

- Is what the Shia await truly from the family of the Seal of the Prophets and Messengers, Muhammad (sws), who came with the Final Divine Scripture (the Holy Quran) to preserve the others, and therefore, establish its rule, or is the truth that what the Shia are waiting for is the false Messiah (the Antichrist) who the Jews are waiting for, and therefore, the rule of the line of David?!!
- Undoubtedly, according to the evidence that has appeared before us, there is unequivocal proof that clearly shows that what the Shia are waiting for their Mahdi to do is the same as what the Jews are waiting for their Messiah to do when he appears.
- Since what the Shia are waiting for is not real (as we have previously shown) and what the Jews are waiting for is the appearance of the Antichrist, which is uncontrovertibly real, then:

  What the Shia are waiting for is really the Antichrist that the Jews believe in and which will wreak havoc on the earth and increase the killing therein.

Another question:

Why do the Shia claim that their twelfth imam will implement the law of the line of David and not the Holy Quran, with which the Seal of the Prophets and Messengers, Muhammad (sws), came and which was sent down to preserve all the previous scriptures and to finalize them?!!

What do the Shia find in books other than the Quran that they don't find in it?!!

Without a doubt, this is unequivocal proof that of the Shia (and those like them) disparagement of the Holy Quran with which the Best of the Messengers, Muhammad (sws), came to finalize all the previous scriptures and to be a guiding document, implemented until the Last Day.

To sum up what we have shown so far in one important question, we say:

Can any Muslim of unspoiled human nature and sound mind believe in what the Shia are waiting for after we have explained here in brief?!!

The answer over which there can be no controversy or neutrality is that:

No Muslim of pure nature and sound mind can believe in the likes of what the Shia are waiting for, and that, in addition to what we have shown above, this is considered defamation of Allah (Glorious & Exalted), in terms of His Knowledge, His Justice, and His Wisdom.

(May Allah Almighty protect us from corruption of our nature and minds, and may He—Blessed & Most High—guide us to righteousness, correctness, and all that is true!)

And so on, from among that which the Shia claim and await their so-called imam to do, which defies all logic, in glaring contrast to pure, untainted human nature and purified, righteous souls.

Dire warnings about the Shia belief in the Imamate, in general, and the twelfth Imam whose emergence from hiding is awaited, in particular

1. We have shown previously that the Mahdi, who the Shia claimed to be their twelfth imam, is not real; he does not exist.
2. The idea of the Mahdi (the twelfth imam) to the Shia sect, whose emergence from hiding they await, is in reality: a metaphor for the rise of the state of Israel.[17]

We have mentioned previously that the founder of this sect was Abdullah ibn Saba', the Jew, whose existence has been established in the books of the Shia themselves, and therefore, the Shia scholars have no way to deny it, either by lying, perfidy, falsification, or slander.

Or it is that the idea of the Mahdi (the twelfth imam) could be a metaphor for the Antichrist,[18] who the Jews are waiting to follow.

And the proof of that is that:

- The Shia, as we have shown, claim that the twelfth imam (their awaited Mahdi), who is known as al-Qa'im, will judge by the laws of the line of David, and not by the Quran—and this is what the Jews insist—in order to establish their state (Israel), and therefore, to rule by the laws of the line of David.
- The Shia, as we have shown, claim that, when their twelfth imam emerges from hiding, he will finish off the Arabs, from whom the prophet of the endtimes, Muhammad (sws), was sent by the Choice and Knowledge of Allah Almighty (for the Jews had been waiting for another prophet of whom the Torah had foretold and of whom the Messiah, Jesus, peace be upon him, had brought glad tidings, but they expected him to be from among them, as had many of the prophets sent before them).
- This is the dream of the Jews: to finish off the Arabs—those who were chosen by Allah Almighty that from them might come the Seal of the Prophets and Messengers, the trustworthy prophet, Muhammad (sws).
- The Shia claim that when their twelfth imam emerges, he will destroy the *qibla* of the Muslims (the Holy Mosque of Mecca) and then destroy the Prophet's Mosque in Medina. This is the dream of the Jews, besides returning to Yathrib (pre-Islamic Medina) from which they were banished at the hand of Prophet Muhammad (sws) because they violated their treaty and covenant with him.
- The Shia sect chose for itself twelve imams, and this is exactly the same number as the tribes of Israel. In fact, the Shia were not content with only that. They called themselves the "Twelvers," taking that number, which represents the number of the tribes of Israel, as a good omen.[19]
- The Shia sect hate the Angel Gabriel (peace be upon him), who is entrusted with the Revelation from above, and this is one of the traits of the Jews,[20] which is why Allah Almighty rebuked them (the Jews) by saying in His Perfect Book (the Holy Quran),

---

[17] *Lillahi, Thumma lit-Taareekh (For Allah, Then for History)*, by al-Sayyid Hussain al-Musawi
[18] Ibid.
[19] Ibid.
[20] Ibid.

﴿قُلْ مَنْ كَانَ عَدُوًّا لِجِبْرِيلَ فَإِنَّهُ نَزَّلَهُ عَلَىٰ قَلْبِكَ بِإِذْنِ اللَّهِ مُصَدِّقًا لِمَا بَيْنَ يَدَيْهِ وَهُدًى وَبُشْرَىٰ لِلْمُؤْمِنِينَ * مَنْ كَانَ عَدُوًّا لِلَّهِ وَمَلَائِكَتِهِ وَرُسُلِهِ وَجِبْرِيلَ وَمِيكَالَ فَإِنَّ اللَّهَ عَدُوٌّ لِلْكَافِرِينَ﴾

It means, {"**Say** (O Muhammad), '**Whoever is an enemy to Gabriel** (let him die in his fury), **for indeed he has brought it** (this Quran) **down to your heart by Allah's Permission, confirming what came before it** (i.e., the Torah and the Gospel) **and guidance and glad tidings for the believers.** * **"Whoever is an enemy to Allah, His Angels, His Messengers, Gabriel and Michael, then verily, Allah is an enemy to the disbelievers."**}
[Al-Baqarah 2: 97-98]

All of this shows clearly the hidden relationship between the Shia and the Jews, which explains a lot of the fierce struggle between them to eliminate the Muslims, the followers of the Seal of the Messengers, Muhammad (sws), the adherents of his Sunnah, and the followers of his noble companions after him.

The Mahdi according to the followers of Prophet Muhammad's (sws) Sunnah

Here we will summarize the creed of the adherents of the Sunnah of Prophet Muhammad (sws) about the Mahdi as the Prophet (sws) informed us (not how the Shia invented it in accordance with their prejudice towards Arabs and the people of the Sunnah of Prophet Muhammad, sws). He will be:

- A righteous man from the line of the Messenger of Allah (sws), from the descendants of his daughter, Fatima (may Allah be pleased with her).
- The birth of the Mahdi and his acknowledgement as the caliph of the Muslims will take place soon before the beginning of the Last Day at the End of Time, before the descent of the Messiah, Jesus, son of Mary (peace be upon him).
- The name of the Mahdi will be: Muhammad ibn Abdullah, the same name as Prophet Muhammad (sws).
- The Mahdi, Muhammad ibn Abdullah, will assume the position of caliph of the Muslims after his leadership has been acknowledged between the *rukn* (corner) and the *maqam* (the station of Abraham) at the Holy Kaäba, and he will establish the laws of Islam (the law to finalize all laws). He will judge by the Quran and revive the Sunnah of the Best of all People, Prophet Muhammad (sws).
- The Mahdi will expand the Islamic liberation of lands and will work to implement the injunctions of Islam, filling the world with fairness and equity after it had been filled with tyranny and oppression.
- The Mahdi, Muhammad ibn Abdullah, will cooperate with the Messiah, Jesus (peace be upon him) to kill the Antichrist (the false messiah who claims divinity) in whom the Jews will have believed.
- Then, in the end, the Mahdi will die and be prayed over. In this, he will be like any of the Muslims.

Though we do not wish to end this section, we will ask but one final question:

- If we were to learn what the Shia believe about the Mahdi and the fables and legends they have made up about him (stemming from their belief in the imamate, as we have shown previously), it would clash with the lowest levels of reason, but if we were to learn what the adherents of the Sunnah of our beloved prophet, Muhammad (sws) believe about this Mahdi, the sound mind would not find the least clash with it:

So which would the person of untainted human nature, a purified soul, and a discerning mind accept?!!

And what does that prove?!!

The answer for which there can be no neutrality, alternative or controversy is:

What the adherents of the Sunnah of our beloved prophet, Muhammad (sws), hold, in terms of sound, upstanding beliefs, is what someone of unsullied human nature would accept, what righteous souls would agree with, and what wise minds would not find the least resistance to.

All of this proves that the truth is what the trustworthy prophet, Muhammad (sws), came with, and what the adherents of his Sunnah hold fast to after him, inviting the people to it until the Day of Judgment.

And all praise is due to Allah Almighty for the blessing of Islam, and all praise is due to Him for the gift of guidance and righteousness.

Shia Beliefs, Summarized

This point we will handle briefly, as follows:

The Shia have comprised in their folds a way of thought and belief that is more dangerous than any other renegade sect that has strayed from Allah's Straight Path and the righteous example of His prophet, Muhammad (sws).

The Shia borrowed in their thought and belief from the Qadriyyah, who denied fate, and the Jahmiyyah, who denied the Attributes of Allah (Mighty & Majestic) and claimed that the Quran was created (as opposed to the uncreated Word of God, which it is).

They borrowed from the Sufi sect through its creed of monism, universalism, and petitioning the deceased in their graves for help.

They borrowed from the Khawarij sect and its threat to declare Muslims to be disbelievers.

They borrowed from the Murji'ah sect when they (the Shia) claim that the love of Ali (may Allah be pleased with him) is a good deed that cannot be decreased by a bad deed.[21]

All of this clearly shows the enormity of the abominable message and corrupt beliefs these Shia (and those of their ilk) follow.

And all praise is due to Allah Almighty for the blessing of Islam, and all praise is due to Him for the gift of guidance and righteousness.

---

[21] *Al-Shia, Shahideen `alaa Anfusihim (The Shia, Testifying Against Themselves)*, by Dr. Diyaa' al-Din al-Kaashif

The Shia and the Legalization of Prostitution (*Mut`a* Marriage), with Refutation

The Shia have claimed the permissibility of a type of marriage called *mut`a*, which means "enjoyment," or prostitution; indeed, they recommend it as much as possible. They have called for it with the loudest voice, violating the authentic, authoritative saying of Allah's Messenger (sws), in blatant violation of the sanctity of the prohibitions of Allah (Mighty & Majestic).

Allah (Glorified & Exalted) did not lay down this law (concerning *mut`a* marriage) as an eternal law to be implemented until the coming of the Hour, due to the great harm and serious corruption that would result therefrom.

Allah's Messenger (sws) would not have permitted what is called *mut`a* marriage as a law to be acted upon by Muslims until the coming of the Hour, and that is because the source of the law with which Prophet Muhammad (sws) came was the Wise, Divine Creator: Allah (Glorious & Exalted), Who sent him with upstanding legislation, to bring His slaves out of the darknesses and into the light.

As a result, the permission for *mut`a* marriage was only for a limited period of time, as a matter of urgent need, to ease the hardship in the beginning. Thereafter, it was banned forever until the coming of the Hour. That was due to the harm and corruption it would cause, the loss and confusion of patrimony, the lack of family stability, and therefore, the lack of social stability as a whole.

The truth of what we have said is shown in a hadith from the Messenger of Allah (sws), in which he says,

»يا أيها الناس إني قد كنت آذنت لكم في الاستمتاع من النساء، وأن الله قد حرّم ذلك إلى يوم القيامة – أي صار محرّمًا من الله تعالى بعد أن مُحلّلًا منه–، فمن كان عنده منهن شيء فليخل سبيله، ولا تأخذوا مما آتيتموهن شيئًا«

It means, "**Oh people, I was going to permit you to seek the enjoyment (*mut`a*) of women, but Allah has prohibited that until the Day of Judgment** (meaning: it has become prohibited by Allah Almighty after it had been permitted by Him), **so whoever has any of them** (*mut`a* wives), **let them go** (divorce them), **but do not take any of what you gave them** (as *mahr*, or dowry)."
[Reported by Muslim]

As for the permissibility of *mut`a* marriage during one limited period of time, during the age of Prophet Muhammad's (sws) mission, the significance of that will become clear in the following way:

Zina, or extra-marital sex, was widespread and open in pre-Islamic Arabian society and elsewhere before the coming of Prophet Muhammad (sws) with the Final Message from Allah (Blessed & Most High), since it was the time of ignorance (before Islam) with all its corruption, especially in such a hot climate which advances puberty and stirs up the sexual instincts.

Then, after the coming of Prophet Muhammad (sws) with the Message and the traveling of the Islamic army in battle after battle, over long days and months, defending Islam and protecting it from the onslaught of its enemies, which made it too much for the Arab to handle—to restrain his desire and hold back his natural instinct towards women for such a long time after that had been so easy for him most of the time (by way of having many wives or because extra-marital affairs were so widespread before the coming of Islam and the prohibition of them) before the coming of Islam—and it was really hard on him.

Consequently, this urgent need was eased by permitting *mut`a* marriage which was allowed in the time before Islam, but that was only for a limited amount of time until it became prohibited eternally until the coming of the Hour.

Thus, the permissibility of *mut`a* marriage resembled what is called 'gradual legislation,' as was the case with alcohol, which was also among the habits of the Arabs and others in the days of ignorance before the coming of Islam, when they used to drink alcohol like water, or even more, until Islam came and prohibited intoxicating substances of all sorts, for all time to come, until the coming of the Hour.

However, it is from the wisdom of Islamic legislation that alcohol was not banned all at once as a means of easement from Allah (Blessed & Most High), of compassion, and of mercy towards His slaves. Hence the gradual nature of the prohibition until it became forbidden to pray while drunk and incoherent (in other words, one is not allowed to pray when one has been drinking and has lost his reason, due to the loss of awareness). This closely resembles the prohibition of drinking alcohol before the time of the obligatory prayer due to the loss of awareness and the impairment of reason, until it became impermissible thereafter to imbibe and drink it, whether it was time for the prayer or near to it or at any other time, and whether the intoxicating substance was a lot or a little.

- The Islam which is the law of the Most Beneficent did not neglect to prohibit what is known as *mut`a* marriage permanently. It did so from the lips of the one who came with it, inviting people to it, Muhammad (sws), and that was a protection from Allah (Blessed & Most High) for the Islamic nation from the vice of *zina*, or extra-marital sex, and a shield for them against getting mired in such a quagmire.

From what we have shown, it is clear that *mut`a* marriage became prohibited permanently, and no one advised it but for two reasons:

1. Either he was unaware of what had been established authoritatively from Allah's Messenger (sws) about his prohibition of what Allah Almighty had forbidden in terms of *mut`a* marriage, permanently, until the coming of the Hour.

    As testament to that fact: this type of marriage (known as *mut`a* marriage) used to take place during the time of Abu Bakr and Umar when they still did not know of its prohibition, but as soon as the Commander of the Faithful, Umar ibn al-Khattab, learned that this type of marriage was prohibited after it had been allowed for a period of time, he began to forbid it.

    And there is nothing strange about one of the companions not knowing about any of the laws for a period of time, since not all of the noble companions accompanied Prophet Muhammad (sws) all the time; rather, some of them would go to work and then come to learn from Allah's Messenger (sws) and some of them Prophet Muhammad (sws) would send on missions and into battles. Yet others would stay to learn from him or otherwise do as we have said before. So the companions of Prophet Muhammad (sws) used to ask amongst themselves about what their messenger (sws) had said while they were gone and they would teach each other, but they might not get to an issue like *mut`a* marriage and the rules related to it until a particular case came up.
2. Or it could be that they were simply following their whims and vain desires, rejecting the Commands of Allah (Mighty & Majestic) and of His messenger (sws). This is exceedingly clear about the Shia since it was founded on wicked principles set by Ibn Saba', the Jew, following what conforms to their vain desires and personal interests.

Thus, we find that the Shia scholars falsely allege that the son born of *mut`a* is better than the son born in permanent wedlock, in order to promote this form of 'marriage' which is repellant to those of pure, upstanding nature and which clashes with those of sound, righteous mind.

The Shia do not stipulate any specific number of women that can be contracted into a *mut`a* marriage at the same time, nor do they stipulate the presence of witnesses or maintenance. In *Furoo` al-Kaafi wa al-Tahdheeb* (one of the standard Shia references), it says that *mut`a* marriage is not dissolvable by divorce, and it does not have any inheritance rights, for it is a rental contract.

To what extent are women humiliated in the light of Shia beliefs, with its abominable message and corrupt legislation??

Could those who promote this illegitimate form of 'marriage' from among the Shia scholars and jurists condone it for their womenfolk and accept it for themselves??

Certainly not. No one could accept this type of 'marriage' except swine who do not have any sense of protectiveness over their women.

We can prove this point with those who call for the likes of this 'marriage' (known as *mut`a* marriage) from among the Shia scholars themselves and likewise their jurists and people of high position and status within the ranks of Shia society, since they reject this type of 'marriage' for their own daughters. They merely permit it for the rest of the girls and women of Shia society since they find therein a crucial means to satisfy their desires, ambitions, and sexual instincts.

In other words, Shia scholars and jurists, and other men of rank and status, use the rest of the masses of Shia society as a means of satisfying their sexual needs through their women, by way of calling for this wicked fornication (known as *mut`a* marriage) which they reject for their own daughters and refuse for their own mothers. Reality bears witness to this fact, for this is a true story, as shown in some of what we have mentioned, and it goes as follows:

A Sunni (one of the followers of the Sunnah of our beloved prophet, Muhammad, sws) argued with a Shiite over *mut`a* marriage: is it permissible or prohibited?

The Sunni presented the authentic, authoritative hadiths from Prophet Muhammad (sws) showing his prohibition of *mut`a* marriage, permanently, until the coming of the Hour, while the Shiite said it is permissible according to the sayings of Shia scholars and jurists.

So the two young men agreed to ask al-Kho'i, one of the Shia scholars. The Sunni boy asked him what he says about *mut`a* marriage: is it permissible or is it forbidden?

Al-Kho'i looked at him, for he sensed something behind the question, so he asked him, "Where do you live?"

The Sunni boy replied, "I live in Mosul, but I have been staying here in Najaf for about two months."

Al-Kho'i said to him, "So you are Sunni, then?"

The boy replied, "Yes."

Al-Kho'i said in response to his question, "*Mut`a* to us (in Shia jurisprudence) is permissible, and to you (in Sunni jurisprudence) is prohibited."

So the Sunni boy said to him (advancing towards him), "I have been here for almost two months as a stranger in your lands, so why haven't you married me to your daughter that I might enjoy her until I return to my family?"

Al-Kho'i stared at him for a little while and then said, "I am a *sayyid* (a noble descendent of Prophet Muhammad, sws). That is forbidden for a *sayyid*, and permitted for the Shia masses."

Then both young men rose, and it was not long before the Shiite boy exploded in a rage, saying (about the Shia jurists and scholars), "You criminals! You permit yourselves to enjoy our daughters, and you tell us it is permitted and that you are drawing near to Allah by doing so, but you forbid us to enjoy your daughters??"

And he began to curse and hurl insults, and he swore that he would become a Sunni[22] (the people of the Sunnah of our beloved prophet, Muhammad, sws).

From this true testimony, the enormity of what the Shia call for and promote (namely, *mut`a* marriage) becomes clear, and it is repellant to anyone of sound human nature and a pure, righteous soul.

The form of marriage approved of by Islam and condoned by Allah (Blessed & Most High) for this final nation (that of Prophet Muhammad, sws) is that which protects its stability, which is achieved because one of the conditions of its validity is that the individual aims for permanence in his marriage, not just to fulfill his desire and satisfy his needs at a particular time, and not refusing to acknowledge the consequences of that in terms of vagrancy for his progeny and helplessness (as in *mut`a* marriage).

Had Islam not forbidden the type of 'marriage' known as *mut`a* marriage, which does not stipulate the presence of witnesses, financial provision, or stability, it would have been possible for us to see the vast majority turning away from the marriage which achieves family stability, and therefore, stability for society as a whole, as well as for the good of mankind, to the type of 'marriage' (*mut`a* marriage) which does not have the least factors of stability and uprightness.

And from what we have presented briefly so far, it has become clear to us that:

What is known as *mut`a* marriage, as claimed and promoted by the Shia, is nothing but obscene fornication, and it has been prohibited by Allah's Messenger (sws), permanently, until the coming of the Hour, in a final law that abrogates any laws before it that permitted it, as a deep solution for eradicating the vice of extra-marital sex, and to stop its spread.

If someone were to say that *mut`a* marriage happened after the death of Prophet Muhammad (sws), that could only be explained to be someone who had not yet heard of the permanent prohibition of such a marriage, someone whom the religious ruling had not yet reached, especially since, at that time, the Muslims were busy with the task of spreading the religion of Allah Almighty (Islam) throughout the world, so they would have to teach each other the religious rulings because there was no means of communication at that time which would allow them to reach each other quickly.

All of this can be sorted out by going back to the authenticated, authoritative hadiths from Prophet Muhammad (sws) through whom people of sound human nature, pure souls, and righteous minds can find guidance.

Therefore, it is clear to see that: the adherents of the Sunnah of our beloved prophet, Muhammad (sws), are the keepers of the truth and its followers.

So, all praise is due to Allah Almighty for the blessing of Islam, and all praise is due to Him for the gift of guidance and righteousness.

---

[22] From the book, *Lillahi, Thumma lit-Taareekh* (*For Allah, Then for History*), by al-Sayyid Hussain al-Musawi

The Shia Belief about *Khums* (the Official Share of the Spoils of War), and Why It Is Incorrect

The Shia made up the innovation of the imamate, as a founding belief of their sect, and they claimed that their imams numbered twelve, but they did not leave it at that. In fact, they went too far. Here is al-Khomeini saying, "Our imams have a station that cannot be reached, neither by a cherished angel, nor by a prophet sent." The Shia also claim that those imams have super powers and that they know the unseen...and so on, from their shocking claims.

The Shia say that their twelfth imam is their last imam, but he has been in hiding, underground, for over one thousand years, and will emerge again at the end of time.

Therefore, the Shia are waiting for him to come out of the place they claim he is hiding in.

However, the Shia have come up with a clever phrase through this story which no sane person could ever believe, in order to collect vast amounts of money for the sake of this claim, by saying that collecting it is only for the hidden imam's awaited return.

As a result, those in high religious positions among the Shia have taken the *Khums*, or one-fifth, of all acquisitions by reason of collecting it for someone alleged to have been in hiding for over one thousand years.

However, the truth is that these large amounts of money they collect, together with the permission they give themselves to engage in what is called *mut'a* marriage—which is, in reality, nothing more than sexual permissiveness (due to Prophet Muhammad's, sws, prohibition of it)—are considered the most prominent pleasures of this short, temporary world whose inhabitants have been deluded by it.

The burning question, therefore, would be:
If the Shia claim that their imams are better than the prophets and messengers, and if the prophets and messengers did not need anyone to collect such large sums of money for them, or any money for that matter, and regardless of that fact, they were helped and supported by Allah (Blessed & Most High), and He made them a reason for His creation to be guided and reformed on earth, then how do the imams, who, according to the beliefs of the Shia, are better than the prophets and messengers and of higher status, need any of this money which the Shia scholars have collected for them?!!

How much longer will they continue to collect these enormous amounts of money?!!
And what does that prove?!!

Without a doubt, in addition to the Shia claims and beliefs that sound human nature and righteous minds cannot accept, we find a glaring, obvious contradiction in this, which proves its objectionable nature and falseness.

In contrast to the beliefs the Shia claim, we find that the creed of the adherents of the Sunnah of Prophet Muhammad (sws) is a pure and clear creed. It does not contain the least conflict or contradiction, which proves that they are the keepers of the truth which the chosen, trustworthy prophet, Muhammad (sws), came to proclaim.

Contradictions about the Shia (and those of their ilk)

The many, many contradictions the Shia (and those of their ilk) have run into are proof of their objectionable message, and these are unequivocal evidence of the falseness of their beliefs.

Among the examples of the contradictions the Shia have produced are:

First: The Shia have expelled the wives of Prophet Muhammad (sws) from his family (*Ahl ul-Bait*); they do not consider them to be a part of the family of Prophet Muhammad (sws). This is, without a doubt, an atrocious offense.

The Holy Quran directly addresses the wives of the prophets and describes them as family. Examples include:

> A. When Sarah, the wife of Allah's prophet, Abraham/Ibrahim (peace be upon him), was given the glad tidings that she would bear a son whose name would be Isaac, she was astonished that she would give birth when she and her husband had both already reached old age, so the messengers of Allah Almighty (who had been sent to Abraham, peace be upon him) said to her in this situation that which is recorded in the Holy Quran, in the Words of Allah Almighty,
>
> ﴿قَالُوا أَتَعْجَبِينَ مِنْ أَمْرِ اللَّهِ رَحْمَةُ اللَّهِ وَبَرَكَاتُهُ عَلَيْكُمْ أَهْلَ الْبَيْتِ إِنَّهُ حَمِيدٌ مَجِيدٌ﴾
>
> which means, {**They said, "Do you wonder at the Decree of Allah? The Mercy of Allah and His Blessings be on you, oh the family** (*ahl ul-bait*, of Abraham). **He** (Allah) **is All-Praiseworthy, All-Glorious."**}[Hud 11: 73]
>
> Therefore, this proves that the wives of the prophets are family, as proved in the address of the Holy Quran to them and the description of them as *Ahl ul-Bait* (members of the household).
>
> B. Likewise, the address in the Holy Quran (the Word of Allah Almighty, Preserved) directed toward the wives of the Prophet (sws) when he ordered them to stay in their homes, forbade them from displaying their beauty (and thence, the order and prohibition were extended to all believing women), and described them as *Ahl ul-Bait*. In the Words of Allah Almighty,
>
> ﴿إِنَّمَا يُرِيدُ اللَّهُ لِيُذْهِبَ عَنْكُمُ الرِّجْسَ أَهْلَ الْبَيْتِ وَيُطَهِّرَكُمْ تَطْهِيرًا﴾
>
> which means, {**Allah wishes only to remove the evil deeds from you, oh members of the family, and to purify you thoroughly.**}[Al-Ahzab 33: 33]

And there are other noble verses that would further demonstrate what we have here shown.

We conclude this disgraceful contradiction into which the Shia (and those like them) have dug themselves with a question to clarify the enormity of the lies in their false accusations, which goes as follows:

Don't the Shia consider Fatima (may Allah be pleased with her)—the daughter of Prophet Muhammad (sws)—from *Ahl ul-Bait*?

Answer: Of course, they do.

So what do they consider her mother, Khadija (may Allah be pleased with her), who was one of the wives of Prophet Muhammad (sws)?!!

Answer: Most certainly, the Shia consider her to be a part of *Ahl ul-Bait*, the family of Prophet Muhammad (sws), since no reasonable person would divide the mother from her daughter, saying that the mother was not from *Ahl ul-Bait*, but the daughter was from *Ahl ul-Bait*. This would be impossible for anyone to claim but an ignorant despiser.

Then, as long as Khadija (may Allah be pleased with her), the wife of Prophet Muhammad (sws) was from his family, the rest of the wives of Prophet Muhammad (sws) must be from his family.

Second: The Shia have said a vile, objectionable thing, namely: that their imams (the twelve imams) have super powers, that they know the unseen, and that the whole universe is under their control.

(May Allah—Mighty & Majestic—be exalted high above such false allegations, abominable insolence, and blatant disbelief!)

Therefore, Ali ibn Abi Talib possesses such falsely alleged powers according to the ridiculous fables of the Shia and what they ascribe to him.

The Shia claim falsely and erroneously that the Rightly-Guided Caliphs, or successors, of Allah's Messenger (sws) were hypocrites, and at their head, Abu Bakr and Umar, which leads us to a question which would clearly show the enormity of the contradiction in such an insidious offense. It is as follows:

If Ali ibn Abi Talib had the powers the Shia claim about their imams, then what made him pledge his allegiance to Abu Bakr al-Siddiq and then Umar ibn al-Khattab, then Uthman ibn `Affan as caliphs, one after the other, if he believed them to be hypocrites as the Shia (and those like them) claim falsely and slanderously?!!

Was it weakness or was he afflicted with the hypocrisy the Shia falsely and slanderously claim they were afflicted with?!!

Would any reasonable person pay any attention to such disgraceful, fallacious nonsense?

What does that mean??

Answer: Of course not. All of this is but proof of the incorrectness of the false allegations and blatant heresy of the Shia, to such an extent that they have become an exact copy of the current religion of the Christians, who make the Messiah a god or one of his 'hypostases,' or 'persons,' and then they show him as weak, incapable, and guileless, especially upon his alleged crucifixion according to their false and slanderous claims.

Also, the Shia have portrayed Ali ibn Abi Talib in a contradictory way, between humiliation and fear, and glory and courage.

Third: We find that the Shia say that whoever pledges allegiance to a false imam is a disbeliever.

Then what do the Shia say about Ali ibn Abi Talib since he pledged his allegiance to Abu Bakr al-Siddiq, Umar, and Uthman when each of them assumed the position of caliph, since the Shia (and those like them) claim, falsely, erroneously, and slanderously, that all of them—Abu Bakr, Umar, and Uthman—were all hypocrites?!!

Would the Shia ascribe to Ali ibn Abi Talib what they would not ascribe to anyone besides Allah Almighty or would they call him a disbeliever according to their beliefs?!!

And what do you say about the allegiance of al-Hassan and al-Hussain to Mu`awiya ibn Abi Sufyan if they did not believe in the validity of his caliphate?!

Undoubtedly, all of these contradictions which must make any rational person of sound human nature and righteous soul, who is devoted exclusively to Allah (Glorious &

Exalted), reject all of this ridiculous prattle and insidious allegations (that the Shia and those of their ilk purport) and follow Allah's Straight Path.

So, all praise is due to Allah Almighty for the blessing of Islam, and all praise is due to Him for the gift of guidance and righteousness.

Fourth: From the full picture of the contradictions and false allegations of the Shia, we see that:

The Shia have reported false narrations alleging the cowardice of Ali ibn Abi Talib and claiming they are true (as in his inability to protect and defend his family).

Among the questions that spring to mind to show part of the confusion and contradiction the Shia are perpetually in, there are as follows:

Could someone who was not qualified for minor leadership, seeing as how he was incapable of protecting and defending his family (according to the false narrations of the Shia which they claim are authentic), be more deserving of major leadership (imamate)?!

Answer: Of course not.

Indeed, the Shia narrations show Ali ibn Abi Talib refusing the imamate, saying, "Leave me and look for someone else."
The question here is:

Wouldn't what Ali ibn Abi Talib said (according to the Shia) have been considered refusal of an Order from Allah Almighty which had been made obligatory on him?!

Answer: Of course, it would have.

Consequently, wouldn't the answer we can infer from the questions we have raised be considered proof of the enormity of the contradiction the Shia sect (and those like them) have gotten themselves into and a removal of the deceptive mask, the insolence, and the lies?!

Answer: Of course, it would.

So, all praise is due to Allah Almighty for the blessing of Islam, and all praise is due to Him for the gift of guidance and righteousness.

Fifth: Among the contradictions the Shia (and those like them) are perpetually in are:

They say that Abu Bakr al-Siddiq (the first caliph after Allah's Messenger, sws) and Umar ibn al-Khattab (the second caliph after Allah's Messenger, sws) are two of Quraysh's idols.

(May Allah Almighty preserve us from such obvious slander and protect us from it.)

As such, we would like to raise a simple question: to those of wisdom and understanding, to anyone with a beating heart and a pure, righteous nature, to those who are devoted exclusively to Allah Almighty, without any partisanship, fanaticism, or nationalism, to those who really want the truth and reject falsehood. And it is as follows:

Isn't Prophet Muhammad (sws) the Seal of the Prophets and Messengers?!

Answer: Of course, he is.

Isn't Prophet Muhammad (sws) the best representative of the Commands of Allah Almighty and the directives of His pure, unadulterated religion (Islam)?!

Answer: Of course, he is.

Would Prophet Muhammad (sws) condone any amount of disbelief when he is the one who came to bring complete, sincere worship of only Allah (Glorious & Exalted)?!

Answer: Certainly not.

Didn't Prophet Muhammad (sws) marry into the families of Abu Bakr and Umar ibn al-Khattab, and indeed, marry both of his own daughters, one after the other (when the first passed away) to Uthman ibn `Affan?!

Answer: Yes, he did.

To proceed:
Would Prophet Muhammad (sws) condone marrying into a family of disbelievers, as when Ali ibn Abi Talib refused to marry the daughter of Abu Jahl, the disbeliever?!

Answer: Certainly not.

Would Prophet Muhammad (sws) condone disbelief in his own home?!!

Answer: Certainly not.

Would Prophet Muhammad (sws) agree to marry his daughter to a disbeliever?!

So what do the Shia (and those like them) think when Prophet Muhammad (sws) married his daughters, one after the other to Uthman ibn `Affan (who the Shia claim is a disbeliever)?!!

Therefore, what shall we conclude from the likes of these questions and others?!
Without a doubt, what we should conclude from this is: that the truth is one, decisive and clear, and falsehood is numerous, contradictory, and constantly repeated; and that the allegations and beliefs of the Shia (and those of their ilk) are pure lies that no one of sound mind could accept.
Such false claims and erroneous concoctions are the result of an old, malicious plan, based externally on attacking the noble companions and others, but on the inside, it is based on attacking the Holy Quran and the Sunnah of the trustworthy prophet, Muhammad (sws), because the noble companions are the link to the Quran and to the pure prophetic tradition.
It is also based secretly on attacking Prophet Muhammad (sws) until they say:
If the companions of the Messenger (sws) are of this fabricated description the Shia (and those of their ilk) have made up, then their companion and teacher (Prophet Muhammad, sws) must be just like them.
Allah forbid that Prophet Muhammad (sws), his noble companions, and his pure and noble wives should be of that false description that the Shia invented!
So, all praise is due to Allah Almighty for the blessing of Islam, and all praise is due to Him for the gift of guidance and righteousness.

Sixth: Among the contradictions the Shia (and those of their ilk) are mired in is that they say Prophet Muhammad (sws) described Abu Bakr as 'al-Siddiq' (the readily believing one) because he used to believe that Prophet Muhammad was a magician.

(Verily to Allah we belong and to Him we shall return.)

Who in their right mind would believe and condone such a lowdown, dirty thing to say?!
Hasn't Allah Almighty granted us reason to distinguish between good and evil, correct and faulty, decent and inferior?!!
Answer: Of course, He has.
Therefore, why do we not use this reason that Allah Almighty has given us and employ it in thinking about the false claims, allegations, and doctrines the enemies of Islam promote that do not sound right at all to those of pure, sound nature?!!
If what the Shia (and those of their ilk) claim is correct, then why didn't Prophet Muhammad (sws) also describe Abu Jahl as 'al-Siddiq' when he claimed that the Prophet (sws) is a magician?!!
Why have the Shia singled out Abu Bakr al-Siddiq for such false allegations?!!
Does Prophet Muhammad's (sws) description of Abu Bakr with this name mean that he (sws) used to fear him, according to the false beliefs of the Shia?! Or does it mean that Prophet Muhammad (sws) was not good at describing?!!
Undoubtedly, the likes of what the Shia claim is merely competing for minds and perplexing plain reason.
If a reasonable person of sound nature heard Prophet Muhammad (sws) describing Abu Bakr as 'al-Siddiq,' then without a doubt, he would know from this description that what Prophet Muhammad (sws) meant behind that description of Abu Bakr was something good. He could not accept any of those other different accusations at all.

Seventh: Among the contradictions the Shia (and those of their ilk) are mired in is:

They allege the disbelief of Aisha (may Allah be pleased with her), the Mother of the Believers.
Without a doubt, such a reprehensible offense is just on account of the wicked plan devised to scheme against Islam and its people.
Aisha (may Allah be pleased with her) related many of the hadiths of Prophet Muhammad (sws) and she transmitted them on his authority, since she (may Allah be pleased with her) lived after Prophet Muhammad (sws) for a long time, during which she transmitted the hadiths that were related from him (sws) before his death.
And among the miracles of Prophet Muhammad (sws) was that he foretold the benefits of the Mother of the Believers, Aisha, for this nation after him, and she turned out to be just like he said, since this entire nation has benefitted from her vast knowledge which was transmitted to us through strong, authentic chains of transmission from the words of Prophet Muhammad (sws), and this was by way of the Mother of the Believers, Aisha (may Allah be pleased with her).
To explain the falseness of this untrue allegation which the Shia (and those of their ilk) have come up with, we would like to raise a few simple questions for those with enlightened minds and sound natures, which go as follows:

Can any rational, rightly-guided person accept that Prophet Muhammad (sws) would be content to marry a disbeliever?!!

Answer: Certainly not.

Therefore, could such an allegation as that claiming the disbelief of Aisha be accepted, despite her marriage to Prophet Muhammad (sws) after he had been made a prophet and had been receiving the Message and had brought Islam to the world?!! Could he (sws) choose her and be content with her as a wife until his death and a mother to the believers until the Day of Judgment?!!
Answer: Certainly not.

As such, what conclusion should we draw from the findings of our answer??

The answer is that: Aisha (may Allah be pleased with her) was the wife of Prophet Muhammad (sws) until he died, and she is the Mother of all the Believers of the nation of Prophet Muhammad (sws), and all the controversy stirred up about her by the Shia (and those of their ilk) is nothing but false allegations, despicable offenses, and incorrect beliefs.

So, all praise is due to Allah Almighty for the blessing of Islam, and all praise is due to Him for the gift of guidance and righteousness.

Eighth: Among the contradictions whose muddy waters the Shia are mired in is:

The Shia (and those of their ilk) claim falsely and erroneously the corruption of the Book of Allah Almighty (the Holy Quran), which was sent down upon the Seal of the Prophets and Messengers, Muhammad (sws). They say that Ali ibn Abi Talib kept the Quran hidden and that it was three times as big as what the Muslims have between their hands today, and that the Quran remained hidden for almost one thousand and two hundred years, or even for an indeterminate period of time, and that it will be with the imam who allegedly is in hiding and will supposedly emerge at the end of time.

Without a doubt, such allegations merely resemble legends and nonsense, since the questions that pop into the mind of the reader of such a wild accusation might be as follows:

What is the point of the Message of Prophet Muhammad (sws), which came to finalize all previous Messages, if the Scripture revealed by Allah Almighty has been corrupted or, according to the lies of the Shia (and those of their ilk), has remained hidden for over one thousand years or for an indeterminate period of time (according to the asinine charges of the Shia and those of their ilk)?!!

Where are the mature, upstanding minds that glorify the Attributes of Allah (Glorious & Exalted), and thus know the Comprehensiveness of His Knowledge and the Perfection and Extent of His Wisdom??

Would Allah Almighty send His prophet, Muhammad (sws), with a deficient scripture to seal all previous Divine Scriptures and to preserve their Essential Message, which has been tasked by Him (Glorious & Exalted) to protect it and to be a light for all the world, a guide for the lost and the confused until the Day of Judgment, just so that, afterwards, it could be corrupted and removed from the righteous and rightly-guided sphere of leading the whole of humanity?!

Answer: Certainly not, no.

And what would be the point of a final message then, if the claim of completely misguiding the entire nation from the Book of their Lord, and therefore from the example of their prophet, for one thousand and two hundred years, or indeed, for an indeterminate period of time?!!

Could anyone of wise, righteous mind and mature, aware heart accept such a serious charge from the Shia (and those of their ilk)?!!

Answer: Certainly not.

So what do such erroneous allegations prove when the Shia have taken them as their doctrine and creed??

Without a doubt, they prove that: such false allegations contain in their folds that which points to wicked plans which tried to plant such wild claims about the corruption of the Quran as a strategy against Islam, out of malice and envy toward its people, since Allah (Glorious & Exalted) vowed to protect His Book (the Holy Quran) as revealed to them, especially since the preservation of the Torah had previously been entrusted to the Jews, but they corrupted it, and then the *Injeel* [the scripture given to Prophet Jesus, peace be upon him], but it was corrupted, changed, and lost, too.

As we have shown previously, the founder of the Shia sect was Ibn Saba', the Jew, and therefore, what we have just mentioned should come as no surprise.

Ninth: Among the murky contradictions the Shia are steeped in is:

The Shia (and those of their ilk) claim that Yazid was the one who killed al-Hussain, despite the fact that there is no evidence of that, yet they still justify such accusations by reasoning that:

As long as al-Hussain was killed during his caliphate, then Yazid was the one who killed al-Hussain.

To refute such a major accusation, we raise an important question, in the following manner:

Wasn't the Mahdi, who the Shia claim is in occultation, hiding underground, their twelfth imam (the imam of the Endtimes), and wasn't his imamate to continue for over one thousand years, even after his occultation?

Answer: Yes, that is what the Shia believe.

Didn't Iraq suffer occupation under the Tatars during the age of the Mahdi whom the Shia claim is in occultation, and didn't they slaughter the Muslims?

Answer: Yes.

Doesn't that mean that the so-called Mahdi of the Shia will emerge from hiding after the Tatars conquered the Abbasid caliphate?!!

Wouldn't this so-called Mahdi of the Shia be considered the one responsible for what happened during his era (according to the claims of the Shia), and shouldn't this be compared to what the Shia claim about Yazid killing al-Hussain just because it happened during the time of his caliphate??

Answer: Yes, it should.

If the matter is not so, according to the Shia, if they say that Yazid was responsible for killing al-Hussain just because it happened during his caliphate, but they do not say the same for their hidden imam, what does that prove??

Undoubtedly, all of this clearly shows the enormity of the glaring contradictions that the Shia (and those of their ilk) are steeped in, in light of these false accusations and erroneous doctrines.

Tenth: Among the contradictions the Shia are mired in is:

The Shia (and those of their ilk) claim that the religion is not complete without the imamate (as they falsely maintain) and that the imams are their twelve so-called imams.

Based on these erroneous claims that the Shia have made up, the position of prophethood and messengership is lower and lesser than the imamate, and the religion was incomplete throughout the period of the Message of Prophet Muhammad (sws) and throughout the caliphates of Abu Bakr, Umar, and Uthman, until the caliphate of Ali ibn Abi Talib came.

In fact, according to the claims of the Shia, the religion was also not complete during the caliphate of Ali ibn Abi Talib because he refused the position of imam and said, according to Shia claims, (دعوني والتمسوا غيري) meaning, "Leave me and find someone else." Therefore, in doing that, he helped to keep the religion incomplete for a longer time.[23]

Could anyone of pure nature and right mind accept such nonsense?!!

Certainly not.

Did the religion remain incomplete after Allah Almighty sent His prophet, Muhammad (sws) to be a seal for the prophets and messengers?!!

Certainly not.

Did the religion remain incomplete after Allah Almighty sent His prophet (sws) with the Miraculous Scripture (the Holy Quran) by which all the previous Divine Scriptures were sealed, and through which the Essential Message of them all was preserved?!!

Certainly not.

Therefore, from whence comes this false creed based on the belief in the imamate, which was not mentioned by Allah (Glorious & Exalted) in His Perfect Book (the Holy Quran) that He promised to preserve until the Day of Judgment, and which was not invented except at the hand of the Shia during that time period??

Undoubtedly, such a false doctrine is nothing but a malicious invention of the enemies of Islam, who cooperated in the founding of this wicked idea which the Shia take as their religion, and a plot from them against Islam, out of hatred towards its people.

However, Allah (Glorious & Exalted) refuses not to let His Light be completed, even if the disbelievers and followers of falsehood hate it.

So, all praise is due to Allah Almighty for the blessing of Islam, and all praise is due to Him for the gift of guidance and righteousness.

---

[23] From the book, *Yulzim al-Raafidah*, with minor editing

Similarities between the Shia and the Jews and the Shia and the Christians

Among the points of resemblance between the Shia and the Jews:

It comes as no surprise to see the obvious resemblance between the beliefs of the Shia and those of the Jews, since, as we have explained in previous sections, the founding of this renegade sect was at the hand of Abdullah ibn Saba', the Jew (may Allah curse him).

Among the points of resemblance between the Shia and the Jews:

1. Shaikh ul-Islam Ibn Taymiyyah (may Allah have mercy on him) said, "Verily, the plight of the Shia is the plight of the Jews; and that is because the Jews said, 'The king shall not come except from the line of David,' and the Shia said, 'The imamate (they have falsely invented) shall not come except from the son of Ali.'"
2. The Jews are plotting to establish the greater state of Israel and this state must be ruled by the laws of the line of David.
   Likewise, the Shia say that when their alleged twelfth imam, called al-Qa'im, emerges from hiding, he will not judge by the law of the Quran, but rather by the law of the line of David.
3. The Jews claim that when the (false) Messiah appears, he will massacre the Muslims; likewise, the Shia say that when their (so-called) twelfth imam (called al-Qa'im) emerges, he will put the Arabs and the Muslims (the adherents of the Sunnah of our beloved prophet, Muhammad, sws) to the sword.
4. Part of the general plot of the Jews is to destroy the Holy Mosque in Mecca (the direction of prayer for Muslims) and to destroy the Prophet's Mosque in Medina.
   Likewise, the Shia claim that upon the emergence of their alleged twelfth imam for whom they have been waiting for over one thousand years, he will destroy the *qibla*, or direction of prayer, of the people of Islam (the adherents of the Sunnah of our beloved prophet, Muhammad, sws): the Holy Mosque of Mecca, and also, he will destroy the Prophet's Mosque in Medina.
5. Also, the Jews hate the Angel of Revelation, Gabriel (peace be upon him)—the best and most noble of the angels before Allah, Blessed & Most High—and treat him with great hostility, and that is because he comes down with the obligations Allah (Glorious & Exalted) has commanded to be revealed to the prophets and messengers.
   Likewise, the Shia say that the Angel Gabriel made a mistake when he came down upon Muhammad (sws) instead of Ali; in fact, there are groups of the Shia that say the Angel Gabriel was a traitor because he brought the Revelation down upon Prophet Muhammad (sws) and they claim that he should have brought it down upon Ali ibn Abi Talib.

As such, it is clear that such false allegations are merely corrupt beliefs, which breed hatred and animosity, or even serious hostility towards the Angel of Revelation, Gabriel (peace be upon him), which is the same as the Jews.

And so on, from the points of resemblance between the Shia and the Jews, which show how agents of falsehood agree with each other and stand side by side.

So, all praise is due to Allah Almighty for the blessing of Islam, and all praise is due to Him for the gift of guidance and righteousness.

Among the points of resemblance between the Shia and the Christians:

The Shia concur with the Christians in the matter of marriage, for the Christians do not have a dowry (*mahr*) for their women; they enjoy them freely.

Similarly, the Shia engage in *mut`a* marriage (which contains no conditions of witnesses or maintenance); they permit it and even promote it.[24]

From the little we have presented, it becomes clear that the creed of the Shia concurs with the beliefs of the enemies of Islam, those who plot against its people and hate them.

As such, this is proof of the falseness of the beliefs and doctrines held by the Shia.

So, all praise is due to Allah for the blessing of Islam, and all praise is due to Him for the gift of guidance and righteousness.

---

[24] *Aqaa'id al-Shia* (with minor editing), compiled by Abdullah ibn Muhammad al-Salafi

How the Jews and Christians are Better than the Shia

In the last chapter, we indicated some of the ways in which the Shia resemble the enemies of Islam: the Jews and the Christians. In this chapter, however, we will demonstrate that, from the disgrace of Allah Almighty on this rebellious sect (the Shia), He made the Jews and Christians superior to them in their beliefs about the people who support the message of their prophets.

If the Jews were asked, "Who are the best people of your nation?"
They would answer, saying, "The companions of Moses."
And if the Christians were asked, "Who are the best people of your nation?"
They would answer, saying, "The disciples of Jesus."
But in complete contrast to this, if the Shia were asked, "Who are the wickedest people of your nation?"
They would reply, "The companions of Muhammad (sws)."[25] Also, both the Jews and the Christians, despite their disbelief and denial of Prophet Muhammad (sws), believe in the truth of the scripture in their hands, and that is despite the obvious corruption of the Torah that Allah's prophet, Moses (peace be upon him), came with, and despite the complete loss of the *Injeel*, with which the Messiah (peace be upon him) came (since, when it was recorded, it was written down in a language other than the language of Revelation, which was one of the reasons it was lost completely, besides the fact that it was not written down at the time of the Messiah).

However, we find that the Shia (and those of their ilk) claim that the Scripture that was sent down upon their prophet, Muhammad (sws) was corrupted, despite the fact that Allah (Blessed & Most High) promised to preserve it until the Day of Judgment.

May Allah preserve us from the slander of the Shia and protect us from it, may He guide us to His Straight Path, and bring us back to the Sunnah of His beloved, the Trustworthy, Muhammad (sws), gently.

So, all praise is due to Allah Almighty for the blessing of Islam, and all praise is due to Him for the gift of guidance and righteousness.

---

[25] From the book, *Aqaa'id al-Shia*, compiled by Abdullah ibn Muhammad al-Salafi, taking from the book, *Manhaj al-Sunnah*, by Shaikh ul-Islam Ibn Taymiyyah

Those Allah Almighty Has Guided to the Way of the Best of All People, Muhammad (sws) and the Followers of *Ahl ul-Sunnah*

Allah (Blessed & Most High) willed to preserve His religion—Islam—despite the plot of His enemies against it, and attempt after attempt to get at it, but Allah (Glorious & Exalted) will complete His Light, even though the followers of falsehood and the disbelievers hate it.

Falsehood is numerous and repetitious, like darknesses.

As for truth, it is only one. It is clear, decisive, and uncontroversial. Truth is the light with which Allah Almighty erases the darknesses.

Because guidance is from Allah (Blessed & Most High), He (Glorious & Exalted) knows best whom to grant this great blessing which is equaled by no other blessing—the blessing of being guided to Him (Glorious & Exalted).

Allah (Glorious & Exalted) willed there to be, among those He has guided to His Straight Path and the righteous example of His prophet (sws), scholars from among the Shia themselves who have learned the truth and revealed the falsehood.

Thus, the *taqiya*, or dissimulation, the Shia engage in no longer has the same importance it had before.

For, Allah (Blessed & Most High) willed that the matter of the Shia be exposed through their scholars and on the lips of their learned men, revealing what was hidden in their hearts, from their abominable message to their corrupt beliefs, and that was due to the truth being explained to them and the dispersion of the fog of falsehood over their eyes.

Among the scholars Allah Almighty has guided to His Straight Path and the followers of the adherents of the Sunnah of our beloved prophet, the Trustworthy, Muhammad (sws), and who have indeed become activists, calling others to this brilliant light and clear truth are the following:

1. Ahmad al-Kasoori, author of *Al-Shia wa al-Tashayoo`*
2. Al-Barqa`i, author of *Kasr al-Sanam*
3. Musa al-Musawi, author of *Al-Shia wa al-Tasheeh*
4. Al-Sayyid Hussain al-Musawi, author of *Lillahi, Thumma lit-Taareekh: Kashf ul-Asraar wa Tabri'at il-A'immat al-At-haar*

And there are many more than those we have mentioned here who have been guided by Allah Almighty to Him and who have been led to the example of His prophet, Muhammad (sws) and his Sunnah.

So, all praise is due to Allah Almighty for the blessing of Islam, and all praise is due to Him for the gift of guidance and righteousness.

Doubts and Misconceptions Stirred up by the Shia, with Brief Refutation

To begin, we would like to briefly respond to the unfounded, vile misconceptions the Shia have before explaining a little of each of them.

When the Shia want to stir up any of these misconceptions, they mostly rely on bringing up fabricated, defective hadiths, with no authentic chain of narration. Then they rely on the ignorance of those they are trying to provoke with such doubts and their inability to respond to them.

As is commonly known and reported about the Shia, they are the biggest liars of all Allah Almighty's creatures when it comes to His Messenger (sws)—except those Allah Almighty has mercy on and guides them—for they work to distort history, with great effort and determination, using whatever methods and wicked means that come to mind, such as:

1. Making things up and lying
2. Manipulating the similarity of names
3. Adding to an incident or leaving something out, according to what they believe will suit the purpose of their distortion
4. Pointing out errors, or in other words, covering up any good points
5. Composing poems to support false historical events and then ascribing them to someone, erroneously and slanderously
6. Planting forged books and letters falsely ascribed to so-and-so or so-and-so, according to what suits their plan and strategy
(Examples of this can be found in the book, *Nahj al-Balaaghah*, which is contested in its chain of transmission and its text.)
7. Using insults disguised as flattery, or in other words, making up an untrue story that may on the surface compliment the person, such that the listener takes in the story and believes it, but then finds that folded up inside, it insults him and as such, he becomes prey to their tricks and deceptions
8. Making films and televisions series (in this age, the age of satellite television and the Internet, which aid in distorting true history and therefore spreading their ideas and beliefs)

And so on of what they come up with day in and day out to execute their plans and schemes, and among the examples of these machinations of the Shia to achieve their devious plans are:

- Citing some of what has come in *History*, by al-Tabari

One of the good things about al-Tabari's *History* is that it does not relate hadiths without the chains of transmission. While we find that the adherents of the Sunnah of our beloved prophet, Muhammad (may the peace and blessing of Allah be upon him) only accept authentic chains of transmission, we find that the Shia and others from the people of innovation in religion take the weak of these chains of transmission when it conforms to their vain desires and ambitions, so that they may find in them what they wish.

They do this despite the fact that Imam al-Tabari himself (and the scholars of Ahlus-Sunnah attest to that) warned readers that in his book that he related information and testimonies without discrimination concerning the chains of transmission; he merely ascribed it to the person who related it. So if what he writes offends the reader or disgusts the listener, it is not from him; rather it is from the narrator. His role (Imam al-Tabari's) is to mention what was narrated to him without investigating the chain of transmission; rather, it is up to the reader to examine that chain.

Among the examples of these narrators of hadith who are weak and unsubstantial, and who cannot be relied upon in their narrations:

- Al-Kalbi: Hadith scholars have classified him as among the abandoned, due to his lying. Also like him is al-Waaqidi, Saif ibn Umar al-Tamimi, and Loot ibn Yahya, who was also called Abu Mukhnaf, as well as others.

The scholars of hadith classified them as those who should be permanently abandoned (*matrookeen*).

All of this enormous effort on the part of the scholars of the adherents of the Sunnah of our beloved prophet, Muhammad (sws), was so that we can distinguish the correct from the faulty, and therefore, separate truth from falsehood.

Suppose, however, that a narration has no chain of transmission (as is the case with a number of the narrations in al-Tabari's *History*), then whenever something is mentioned about the companions of Prophet Muhammad (sws), we must suffice ourselves with the basic working assumption that everyone testifies to, which is that Allah (Glorious & Exalted) has praised them in His Perfect Book (the Holy Quran), and likewise, His Messenger, Muhammad (sws), bore witness to that in his commendation of them in his authentic noble hadiths.

Also, if the matter pertains to what the Shia accuse the Mother of the Believers, Aisha (may Allah be pleased with her) of, slanderously and erroneously, we should suffice ourselves with Allah's (Glorious & Exalted) declaration of her innocence in His Perfect Book (the Holy Quran), and in the context of the verses to be recited until the Day of Judgment. Likewise, there is the testimony of Allah's Messenger (sws) about her and his praise for her, as well as for others of the Mothers of the Believers, the wives of Allah's Messenger (sws), who are not free of the attacks of the Shia and their vicious lies.

In other words, the basic principle is to return to the Book of Allah (Blessed & Most High) and to the authentic, trustworthy hadiths of the Prophet (sws), which can be accurately ascribed to him. Then we must look at the chains of transmission of the narrations mentioned in al-Tabari's *History* and the correct interpretation of them without exaggerating them, according to the source we have, which is the Book of Allah Almighty and the authentic hadiths of Allah's Messenger (sws), without taking some of them and leaving others, so that the full meaning of them may become clear to us.

After presenting a complete refutation of the base, unfounded misconceptions the Shia stir up, we should point out some of the details on how to respond to them, as follows:

1. The Shia have made attacking the companions of the Prophet (sws) a main part of their doctrine, by falsely interpreting some of the verses of the Holy Quran that bear some resemblance to each other, in clear contradiction of the obvious meaning of other unequivocal, unambiguous verses and authentic, authoritative hadiths from the Messenger (sws).

And Allah's Words are true when He says,

﴿هُوَ الَّذِي أَنْزَلَ عَلَيْكَ الْكِتَابَ مِنْهُ آيَاتٌ مُحْكَمَاتٌ هُنَّ أُمُّ الْكِتَابِ وَأُخَرُ مُتَشَابِهَاتٌ فَأَمَّا الَّذِينَ فِي قُلُوبِهِمْ زَيْغٌ فَيَتَّبِعُونَ مَا تَشَابَهَ مِنْهُ ابْتِغَاءَ الْفِتْنَةِ وَابْتِغَاءَ تَأْوِيلِهِ وَمَا يَعْلَمُ تَأْوِيلَهُ إِلَّا اللَّهُ وَالرَّاسِخُونَ فِي الْعِلْمِ يَقُولُونَ آمَنَّا بِهِ كُلٌّ مِنْ عِنْدِ رَبِّنَا وَمَا يَذَّكَّرُ إِلَّا أُولُو الْأَلْبَابِ﴾

It means, {It is He Who has sent down to you (Muhammad) the Book (this Quran). In it are Verses that are entirely clear, they are the foundations of the Book, and others not entirely clear. So as for those in whose hearts there is a deviation (from the truth), they follow that which is not entirely clear thereof, seeking trouble and seeking out its hidden meanings, but none knows its hidden meanings save Allah. And those who are firmly grounded in knowledge say, "We believe in it; the whole of it (both the clear and unclear Verses) are from our Lord." And none receive admonition except men of understanding.}
[Aal `Imran 3: 7]

In the following noble verses we will mention, the reader will see the praise of Allah Almighty of Prophet Muhammad (sws) and his noble companions, and His description of them with many good qualities. These verses we have before us are the Words of Allah Almighty,

﴿مُحَمَّدٌ رَسُولُ اللَّهِ وَالَّذِينَ مَعَهُ أَشِدَّاءُ عَلَى الْكُفَّارِ رُحَمَاءُ بَيْنَهُمْ تَرَاهُمْ رُكَّعًا سُجَّدًا يَبْتَغُونَ فَضْلًا مِنَ اللَّهِ وَرِضْوَانًا سِيمَاهُمْ فِي وُجُوهِهِمْ مِنْ أَثَرِ السُّجُودِ ذَلِكَ مَثَلُهُمْ فِي التَّوْرَاةِ وَمَثَلُهُمْ فِي الْإِنْجِيلِ كَزَرْعٍ أَخْرَجَ شَطْأَهُ فَآزَرَهُ فَاسْتَغْلَظَ فَاسْتَوَى عَلَى سُوقِهِ يُعْجِبُ الزُّرَّاعَ لِيَغِيظَ بِهِمُ الْكُفَّارَ وَعَدَ اللَّهُ الَّذِينَ آمَنُوا وَعَمِلُوا الصَّالِحَاتِ مِنْهُمْ مَغْفِرَةً وَأَجْرًا عَظِيمًا﴾

It means, {Muhammad is the Messenger of Allah, and those who are with him are severe against disbelievers, and merciful among themselves. You see them bowing and falling down prostrate (in prayer), seeking Bounty from Allah and (His) Good Pleasure. The mark of them (i.e. their faith) is on their faces (foreheads) from the traces of (their) prostration (during prayers). This is their description in the Torah. But their description in the *Injeel* (the Book of Prophet Jesus) is like a (sown) seed which sends forth its shoot, then makes it strong, it then becomes thick, and it stands straight on its stem, delighting the sowers—that He may enrage the disbelievers with them. Allah has promised those among them who believe and do righteous good deeds forgiveness and a mighty reward.}
[Al-Fath 48: 29]

In this it is clear that Allah Almighty has praised the noble companions of His prophet (sws), saying that they are:

- Tough on the disbelievers
- Merciful amongst each other
- They worship Allah Almighty Alone, bowing in prayer, and prostrating themselves to Him (Glorious & Exalted), hoping for His Bounty and Good Pleasure.

What we have mentioned is the straightforward meaning of the noble verse; it is what is understood clearly.

The Shia, on the other hand, have refused to stop attacking the companions of Prophet Muhammad (sws), relying on an erroneous interpretation when two verses are similar. They abandon the obvious, straightforward, unequivocal, plain meaning of other verses when it contradicts their vain desires and schemes and does not conform to them.

We find the Shia have said that the word, (مِن) "min," (from, among) in the phrase, (مِنْهُم) "minhum," (among them) in the Words of Allah Almighty,

﴿وَعَدَ اللَّهُ الَّذِينَ آمَنُوا وَعَمِلُوا الصَّالِحَاتِ مِنْهُم مَّغْفِرَةً وَأَجْرًا عَظِيمًا﴾

which means, {**Allah has promised those among them who believe and do righteous good deeds forgiveness and a mighty reward.**}[Al-Fath 48: 29]

expresses enmity, meaning that some of those who believe and do righteous good deeds will receive forgiveness and a mighty reward, while the rest will not have that. What they intend in this, what they are striving and working for is to distort the picture of the noble companions with their fallacious claim stemming from the Shia belief that the companions committed apostasy from Islam and disbelieved, except for three or five of them, or slightly more than that.

Undoubtedly, such a charge is an abominable offense, since:

The truth on which the scholars of Quranic exegesis (*tafseer*) stand is that: (مِن) "min," (of, from, or among) in the phrase, (مِنْهُم) "minhum," does not express enmity as the followers of falsehood claim; rather, it has one of the following two meanings:

A. The first meaning:

The word, (مِن) "min," in the phrase, (مِنْهُم) "minhum," means: "of their type or kind," as in the Words of Allah Almighty,

﴿..... فَاجْتَنِبُوا الرِّجْسَ مِنَ الْأَوْثَانِ﴾

meaning, {**So shun the abomination** (worshipping) ***of idols*, and shun lying speech**}[Al-Hajj 22: 30]

It is not understood from this verse that we should avoid some of the idols and not others; rather, it is understood that we are required to avoid all idols.

The word, (مِن) "min," (of, from, among) has therefore come here with the meaning: "avoid the abomination of the category of these idols."[26]

B. The second meaning:

The word, (مِن) "min," in the phrase, (مِنْهُم) "minhum," may have come to express emphasis, as in the Words of Allah Almighty,

﴿وَنُنَزِّلُ مِنَ الْقُرْآنِ مَا هُوَ شِفَاءٌ وَرَحْمَةٌ لِلْمُؤْمِنِينَ﴾

meaning, {**And We send down *from the Quran* that which is a healing and a mercy to those who believe**}[Al-Israa' 17: 82]

Thus the meaning of the noble verse is that: "the Holy Quran, all of it, is a healing and a mercy to the believers," not that some of its verses are a healing and a mercy, and others are not.[27]

As such, the word, (مِن) "min," here expresses emphasis.

---

[26] *Huqbah min al-Taareekh*—with minor editing—by Shaikh Uthman al-Khamees
[27] Ibid.

From what we have presented herein, the falseness of this base misconception that the Shia have made up becomes clear, and this is a brief example of a definitive refutation of it and unequivocal proof of its erroneous nature, in addition to the straightforward noble verses of which the Holy Quran has told us which confirm our argument.

2. Prophet Muhammad (sws) has said,

«يرد عليّ رجال أعرفهم ويعرفونني، فيذادون عن الحوض، فأقول أصحابي، فيقال إنك لا تدري ما أحدثوا بعدك»

It means, "Men I know and who know me will be presented before me, but they will be removed from the Basin, so I will say, 'My companions!' Yet it will be said, 'Verily, you do not know what they invented after you.'"[28]

Among the other narrations of this noble prophetic hadith is:

«إني على الحوض حتى أنظر من يرد علي منكم، وسيؤخذ أناس دوني، فأقول يا رب مني ومن أمتي، فيقال: أما شعرت ما عملوا بعدك، والله ما برحوا بعدك يرجعون على أعقابهم»

It means, "Verily, I am at the Basin in order to see who is being presented before me, and people will be taken away from me, so I say, 'Oh Lord! [They are] from me and from my nation!' And it is said, 'You do not realize what they have done after you. By Allah, they began after you turning on their heels.'"[29]

As usual, the attackers refuse to cite anything but ambiguous verses of the Holy Quran and noble prophetic hadiths, which allows them to find whatever they want in their incorrect interpretation.

The Shia stopped at the word, (أصحابي) "as-haabi," (my companions) in the first hadith, claiming that this word refers to the companions of Prophet Muhammad (sws), starting with Abu Bakr, Umar, and Uthman, until the last of the companions (may Allah be pleased with them all), as an attack on them, in accordance with the claim that they committed apostasy and disbelief, as stated in their malicious doctrines (those of the Shia and those of their ilk).

Undoubtedly, this allegation particular to the Shia exegesis of the word, (أصحابي) "as-haabi," (my companions) in the first hadith is simply wrong. It is an egregious offense since it contradicts the straightforward noble Quranic verses related concerning the virtues of the noble companions and Allah's (Blessed & Most High) Good Pleasure with them, in addition to contradicting the straightforward noble prophetic hadiths, authentically attributed to him which have been related about the great virtue and honor of the companions (may Allah be pleased with them).

In addition to the straightforward noble Quranic verses and the noble prophetic hadiths which show the great virtue of the noble companions and the praise and commendation Allah (Blessed & Most High) has visited upon them and His Good Pleasure with them, we should point out the following:

---

[28] *Sahih al-Bukhari*
[29] Ibid.

A. The meaning of the word, (أصحابي) "*as-haabi*," (my companions) in the noble hadith is: the hypocrites.

The hypocrites outwardly profess Islam and inwardly disbelieve. They prayed with Prophet Muhammad (sws), but their hearts were empty of faith and submission.[30]

Among those hypocrites are those whom Prophet Muhammad (sws) thought were among his companions, since he didn't know of their hypocrisy, nor did Allah Almighty inform him of that. The proof of this is in the Words of Allah (Glorious & Exalted),

﴿وَمِمَّنْ حَوْلَكُمْ مِنَ الْأَعْرَابِ مُنَافِقُونَ وَمِنْ أَهْلِ الْمَدِينَةِ مَرَدُوا عَلَى النِّفَاقِ لَا تَعْلَمُهُمْ نَحْنُ نَعْلَمُهُمْ سَنُعَذِّبُهُمْ مَرَّتَيْنِ ثُمَّ يُرَدُّونَ إِلَى عَذَابٍ عَظِيمٍ﴾

It means, {**And among the Bedouins round about you, some are hypocrites, and so are some among the people of Medina. They exaggerate and persist in hypocrisy. You** (Muhammad) **know them not; We know them. We shall punish them twice, and thereafter they shall be brought back to a great** (horrible) **torment.**}
[Al-Tawbah 9: 101]

B. The meaning of the word, (أصحابي) "*as-haabi*," (my companions) is that they are the ones who committed apostasy after the death of Prophet Muhammad (sws) and then they died in that state.

After the death of Prophet Muhammad (sws), many of the Arabs committed apostasy and refused to pay the *zakat* (the poor due), so the companions of Prophet Muhammad (sws) went to war against them by order of the first caliph, Abu Bakr al-Siddiq.

Consequently, the meaning of the word, (أصحابي) "*as-haabi*," (my companions) is: those who turned away from Islam, although they had been considered to be among the companions of Allah's Messenger (sws) and although they (the apostates) thought themselves to be among them (the noble companions).[31]

C. The meaning of the word, (أصحابي) "*as-haabi*," (my companions) is: the general meaning of the word, which is "those who accompanied Prophet Muhammad (sws), even if they did not believe in him and follow him."[32]

D. The meaning of the word, (أصحابي) "*as-haabi*," is: Everyone who accompanied Prophet Muhammad (sws) on this path, even if they did not see him, and the proof for this is the narration that includes the word, (أمتي) "*ummati*," (my nation).

The words of Prophet Muhammad (sws), (أعرفهم) "*a`rafhum*," (I know them) also prove this interpretation, for it is explained in another authentic hadith that Prophet Muhammad (sws) will know his nation on the Day of Resurrection from the traces of ablution.

As we have indicated, this brief, simple explanation confirms what has been shown in the straightforward, noble Quranic verses and the other unambiguous, authentic hadiths that have been related concerning the virtues of the noble companions and Allah Almighty's praise of them and Good Pleasure with them.

---

[30] *Huqbah min al-Taareekh*—with minor editing—by Shaikh Uthman al-Khamees
[31] Ibid.
[32] *Ibid.*

Consequently, the falseness of these vile misconceptions invented by the Shia shows itself to be merely a way of attacking Islam and the adherents of the Sunnah of our beloved prophet, Muhammad (sws).

For, the noble companions are the best humanity has known after the prophets and messengers.

Indeed, Allah Almighty has said,

﴿كُنتُمْ خَيْرَ أُمَّةٍ أُخْرِجَتْ لِلنَّاسِ تَأْمُرُونَ بِالْمَعْرُوفِ وَتَنْهَوْنَ عَنِ الْمُنكَرِ وَتُؤْمِنُونَ بِاللَّهِ وَلَوْ آمَنَ أَهْلُ الْكِتَابِ لَكَانَ خَيْرًا لَهُم مِّنْهُمُ الْمُؤْمِنُونَ وَأَكْثَرُهُمُ الْفَاسِقُونَ﴾

It means, {**You** (true believers and followers of the Prophet, sws) **are the best of peoples ever raised up for mankind; you enjoin the good and forbid the evil, and you believe in Allah. And had the people of the Scripture** (Jews and Christians) **believed, it would have been better for them; among them are some who have faith, but most of them are rebellious.**}
[Aal 'Imran 3: 110]

As is common knowledge, this noble verse was revealed to Prophet Muhammad (sws) and his noble companions are those who believed in him, aided him, and supported his mission.

It would be impossible for Allah Almighty to describe the nation of Prophet Muhammad (sws) as the best nation when they practice enjoining the good and forbidding the evil, but then believe in what the Shia claim—that all of the companions (the Emigrants from Mecca and the Helpers in Medina) committed apostasy except for three of them, despite the fact that the companions are the best example as referred to in this noble verse (as indicated above).[33]

Does it make sense that the description, (أمة) "*ummah*," (nation) mentioned in this noble verse only refer to three of the companions?!!

Are these three, who the Shia claim remained steadfast in faith and in their Islam to the exclusion of the others, the ones meant by the word, (أمة) "*ummah*"?!!

Answer: No.

No one says such incoherent things, but someone vicious and malicious, who will spare no effort to introduce a foreign agenda with a wicked plot and a strategy to get at Islam and its adherents.

To conclude the refutation of this misconception the Shia have stirred up, we mention what Ibn Masoud (may Allah be pleased with him) said,

(إن الله نظر في قلوب العباد، فوجد قلب محمد (ص) خير القلوب، فاصطفاه لنفسه، فابتعثه برسالته، ثم نظر في قلوب العباد بعد قلب النبي محمد (ص) فوجد قلوب أصحابه خير قلوب العباد، فجعلهم وزراء نبيه، يقاتلون على دينه)

Meaning, "Verily, Allah looks at the hearts of the slaves, and He found the heart of Muhammad (sws) the best heart, so He chose him for Himself and sent him with His Message. Then, he looked at the hearts of the slaves after the heart of Prophet Muhammad (sws), and He found the hearts of the companions the best of the slaves' hearts, so He made them the ministers of His prophet, fighting for His religion."

---

[33] *Huqbah min al-Taareekh*—with minor editing—by Shaikh Uthman al-Khamees

3. The Shia have said that the companions angered Prophet Muhammad (sws) after the Treaty of Hudaybiyyah with Quraysh, since they returned without performing the lesser pilgrimage (*Umrah*). He ordered the companions to shave their heads and perform the ritual sacrifice, but they did not do as he said, so he (sws) got angry, and therefore, the Shia say that whoever angers the Prophet (sws) cannot possibly be an upright person.

Undoubtedly, what the Shia say in this respect is merely a pessimistically unjust assumption, a lack of understanding, and an unfounded accusation.

In fact, Prophet Muhammad (sws) simply did not know his status in the eyes of his noble companions (may Allah be pleased with them all).

To explain part of what testifies to this fact, we mention what 'Urwa ibn Masoud said in this respect to Quraysh, to clarify what seemed to him to be the situation of the companions with Allah's Messenger (sws) on the Day of Hudaybiyyah. He said,

(أي قوم، والله لقد وفدت على الملوك، ووفدت على قيصر وكسرى والنجاشي، والله ما رأيت ملكًا قط يعظمه أصحابه ما (كما) يعظم أصحاب محمد محمدًا، والله إن تنخم بنخامة إلا وقعت في كف رجل منهم فدلك بها وجهه، وإذا أمرهم ابتدروا أمره، وإذا توضأ كادوا يقتتلون على وضوئه، وإذا تكلموا خفضوا أصواتهم، وما يحدّون النظر إليه تعظيمًا له...).

meaning, "Oh people! By Allah, I have visited kings, and I have visited Caesar (of Byzantium) and Chosroes (of Persia) and the Negus (of Abyssinia), but by Allah, I have never seen a king whose companions revere him as the companions of Muhammad revere Muhammad. By Allah, if he cleared his throat and some spittle fell on one of their sleeves, he would rub his face with it; if he ordered them to do something, they would rush to do it; if he performed ablution, they would practically kill each other to get at the remaining water; and if he spoke, they would lower their voices and look attentively at him in admiration..."

As such, it becomes clear to us that what appeared to happen to the companions (may Allah Almighty be pleased with them), when they hesitated to respond to the command of Allah's Messenger (sws) to shave and sacrifice, was not in the manner of disobedience; rather, it was in hopes that Prophet Muhammad (sws) would change his mind and that Revelation from Allah (Blessed & Most High) would descend upon him that he should enter Mecca. This was out of longing on their part to go to Allah's Sacred House and circumambulate it. That is why they hesitated.

However, when Prophet Muhammad (sws) himself went out, shaved his head and slaughtered his sacrificial animal, they all knew that it was over, that there was no turning back, so they shaved their heads and slaughtered their sacrificial animals, in response to the Command of Allah Almighty and the order of His Messenger (sws),[34] whereupon Allah Almighty sent down upon them His Words,

﴿لَقَدْ رَضِيَ اللَّهُ عَنِ الْمُؤْمِنِينَ إِذْ يُبَايِعُونَكَ تَحْتَ الشَّجَرَةِ فَعَلِمَ مَا فِي قُلُوبِهِمْ فَأَنزَلَ السَّكِينَةَ عَلَيْهِمْ وَأَثَابَهُمْ فَتْحًا قَرِيبًا﴾

It means, {**Indeed, Allah was pleased with the believers when they gave their pledge to you** (Muhammad) **under the tree; He knew what was in their hearts, and He sent down tranquility upon them. And He rewarded them with an imminent victory.**}
[Al-Fath 48: 18]

---

[34] *Huqbah min al-Taareekh*—with minor editing—by Shaikh Uthman al-Khamees

And He (Glorious & Exalted) revealed,

﴿مُحَمَّدٌ رَسُولُ اللَّهِ وَالَّذِينَ مَعَهُ أَشِدَّاءُ عَلَى الْكُفَّارِ رُحَمَاءُ بَيْنَهُمْ تَرَاهُمْ رُكَّعًا سُجَّدًا يَبْتَغُونَ فَضْلًا مِنَ اللَّهِ وَرِضْوَانًا سِيمَاهُمْ فِي وُجُوهِهِمْ مِنْ أَثَرِ السُّجُودِ ذَلِكَ مَثَلُهُمْ فِي التَّوْرَاةِ وَمَثَلُهُمْ فِي الْإِنْجِيلِ كَزَرْعٍ أَخْرَجَ شَطْأَهُ فَآزَرَهُ فَاسْتَغْلَظَ فَاسْتَوَى عَلَى سُوقِهِ يُعْجِبُ الزُّرَّاعَ لِيَغِيظَ بِهِمُ الْكُفَّارَ وَعَدَ اللَّهُ الَّذِينَ آمَنُوا وَعَمِلُوا الصَّالِحَاتِ مِنْهُمْ مَغْفِرَةً وَأَجْرًا عَظِيمًا﴾

It means, {**Muhammad is the Messenger of Allah, and those who are with him are severe against disbelievers, and merciful among themselves. You see them bowing and falling down prostrate** (in prayer), **seeking Bounty from Allah and** (His) **Good Pleasure. The mark of them** (i.e. their faith) **is on their faces** (foreheads) **from the traces of** (their) **prostration** (during prayers). **This is their description in the Torah. But their description in the** *Injeel* (the Book of Prophet Jesus) **is like a** (sown) **seed which sends forth its shoot, then makes it strong, it then becomes thick, and it stands straight on its stem, delighting the sowers—that He may enrage the disbelievers with them. Allah has promised those among them who believe and do righteous good deeds forgiveness and a mighty reward.**}
[Al-Fath 48: 29]

As a result, we can see the pessimistically unjust assumption, the lack of understanding, and the unfounded accusation which is the way of those who attack Islam and who are full of malice towards its adherents.

It is clear that the abominable accusations the Shia have invented about the best people after the prophets and messengers is just another method of slander and lies.

4. The attackers have taken another path besides accusing the best of humanity after the prophets and messengers of Allah Almighty (those whom mankind has never seen a comparable example), and this is by attacking the wives of Allah's Messenger (sws). The Shia have accused the Mother of the Believers, Aisha (may Allah be pleased with her), and likewise, the Mother of the Believers, Hafsa (may Allah be pleased with her), and others, with a vile, heinous charge: the charge of disbelief and apostasy from Islam.

The Shia claim that in this verse,

﴿إِنْ تَتُوبَا إِلَى اللَّهِ فَقَدْ صَغَتْ قُلُوبُكُمَا وَإِنْ تَظَاهَرَا عَلَيْهِ فَإِنَّ اللَّهَ هُوَ مَوْلَاهُ وَجِبْرِيلُ وَصَالِحُ الْمُؤْمِنِينَ وَالْمَلَائِكَةُ بَعْدَ ذَلِكَ ظَهِيرٌ﴾

which means, {**If you two** (Aisha and Hafsa) **turn in repentance to Allah,** (it will be better for you), **your hearts are indeed so inclined** (to oppose what the Prophet, sws, likes), **but if you help one another against him** (Muhammad), **then verily, Allah is his Protector, and Gabriel, and the righteous among the believers, and furthermore, the angels, are his helpers.**}
[Al-Tahrim 66: 4]

there is proof of this vicious claim.

If that is the case, why then do all of the arguments springing forth from their followers come from ambiguous verses of the Holy Quran and not from the unambiguous verses, unless they are just trying to make trouble and interpret them the way they want?

In fact, the argument the Shia make for this vicious claim and abominable affront is focused in the Word of Allah Almighty, (صغت) "*saghat*" (so inclined). They claim that this means: "inclined to disbelief," but there is no doubt that this is a lie, and the scholars of Islam have shown it to be false.

The correct interpretation of the Word of Allah Almighty, (صغت) "*saghat*," is: "inclined away from the truth in this deed, when the deed is wrong," but the meaning is not the disbelief which negates faith, as the Shia have alleged.

Confirmation for what we have said can be found in the unequivocal verses of the Holy Quran, which are those that do not leave room for people like the Shia (and others) to misinterpret them.

Confirmation can also be found for what we have said in the authentic and authoritative sayings of Allah's Messenger (sws).

As for the reason these noble verses were revealed, we refer the reader to any of the reliable volumes of exegesis of the Holy Quran, such as *Tafsir ibn Kathir*.

What we hoped to clarify on this point is that the false allegations of the Shia and what they have invented are an abominable offense.

5. In part of a long hadith, Prophet Muhammad (sws) has said concerning the right of Ali ibn Abi Talib (may Allah be pleased with him),

«من كنت مولاه فعلي مولاه»

"For whomever I was his master (*mawla*)**, Ali is his master** (*mawla*)."
[Related by al-Haakim in *al-Mustadrak*]

As we have indicated previously, those who follow their vain desires use and ignore noble Quranic verses and prophetic hadiths according to their wishes, according to whichever erroneous interpretation suits their intentions.

The Shia have claimed that this part of the hadith just mentioned proves that Ali should have been the caliph after the Messenger, Muhammad (sws), and that the caliph and the *mawla* means the *wali*: the master who must be obeyed.

Undoubtedly, this understanding invented by the Shia is not correct at all, since what Prophet Muhammad (sws) said was said on a certain occasion, completely removed from what the Shia have taken it as, in terms of being the caliph and the *wali*. In fact, the Shia scholars and jurists have made false additions to this authentic hadith to support the varying opinions they have in their interpretations.

The truth is that the reason for the hadith was two events:

The first event:

عن بريدة بن الصحيب رضي الله عنه قال: أرسل خالد بن الوليد إلى النبي محمد (ص) ليرسل إليه من يقبض الخمس، فجاء علي وقبض الخمس، ثم اختار جارية من الخمس ودخل بها، وقال بريدة: وكنت أبغض عليا وقد اغتسل (يعني أنه قد اغتسل بعد أن دخل بالجارية)، فقلت لخالد: ألا ترى إلى هذا؟! فلما قدمنا إلى النبي (ص) ذكرت له ذلك، فقال النبي لبريدة: «يا بريدة، أتبغض عليا؟» فقلت: نعم، فقال النبي (ص): لا تبغضه، فإن له في الخمس أكثر من ذلك»

It means, (On the authority of Buraidah ibn al-Suhayb (may Allah be pleased with him), "Khalid ibn al-Walid sent to Prophet Muhammad (sws) to send him someone to collect the *Khums* (the official share of the spoils of war), so Ali came and collected the *Khums*. Then, he chose a slave-girl from the *Khums* and had relations with her. Buraidah said, 'I hated Ali while he was taking the ritual bath (following sexual relations), so I said to Khalid, "Don't you see that?!" Then, when we went to the Prophet (sws), I mentioned that to him, and the Prophet (sws) said to Buraidha, **"Oh Buraidah, do you hate Ali?"** So I said, "Yes." And the Prophet (sws) said, **"Don't hate him, for he deserves more of the *Khums* than that."**")[35]

In the narration of al-Tirmidhi, (it states) that the Prophet (sws) said to Buraidah,

«من كنت مولاه فعلي مولاه»

meaning, "For **whomever I am his master** (*mawla*), **Ali is his master** (*mawla*)."

The second event:

عن أبي سعيد أن عليًّا منعهم من ركوب إبل الصدقة (لما كانوا في اليمين)، وأمرّ عليهم رجلًا، وخرج إلى النبي ﷺ في مكة، ثم لما أدركه في الطريق إذا أمرّه الذي أذن لهم بالركوب، فلما رآهم ورأى الإبل عليها أثر الركوب، غضب ثم عاتب نائبه الذي جعله مكانه.

قال أبو سعيد: فلما لقينا رسول الله ﷺ، ذكرنا ما لقينا من علي (من الغلظة والتضييق)، وفي رواية أنها كانت حللًا أرادوا أن يلبسوها فمنعهم علي رضي الله عنه من لبسها، فقال رسول الله ﷺ: «مه يا سعد بن مالك (وهو أبو سعيد) بعض قولك لأخيك، فوالله لقد علمت أنه أحسن في سبيل الله»

On the authority of Sa`eed, Ali forbid them to ride the camels from charity (when they were in Yemen), and he placed a man in charge of them and left for the Prophet (sws) in Mecca. Then, when he caught up with him along the way, he found that the one he had placed in charge had given them permission to ride, and when he saw them and saw the signs of being ridden on the camels, he became angry and rebuked his deputy who he had made take his place.

Abu Sa`eed said, "So when we met Allah's Messenger (sws), we mentioned to him what we had experienced from Ali (the mistake and hardship), and in another narration, it had been clothing they wanted to wear which Ali (may Allah be pleased with him) forbade them from wearing, so Allah's Messenger (sws) said, **'Oh Sa`ad ibn Malik** (who was Abu Sa`eed), **some of what you say is for your brother, for by Allah, I have learned that he is better in Allah's Cause.'**" (Ibn Kathir said, "Its chain of narration is good according to the conditions of al-Nasa'i, transmitted by al-Baihaqi and others.)

Ibn Kathir said, "Verily, Ali (may Allah be pleased with him), when the gossip about him increased among that army because he forbid them to use the camels from charity, and his taking back the garments his deputy had given them, the Prophet (sws) addressed the people and declared Ali innocent. He raised his standing and pointed out his virtue to remove what had settled into the hearts of the people."[36]

Consequently, we see that the obviously correct opinion about the saying of Prophet Muhammad (sws),

«من كنت مولاه فعلي مولاه»

meaning, **"For whomever I was his master** (*mawla*), **Ali is his master** (*mawla*)"

is that the meaning of him being his *mawla* is in being his *mawla* in support and love, the opposite of being his enemy.

---

[35] Related by al-Bukhari
[36] *Huqbah min al-Taareekh*—with minor editing—by Shaikh Uthman al-Khamees

As proof of this:

The word, *mawla*, can mean the Lord (Glorious & Exalted), and it can be used to mean the owner, the provider, the protector, the friend, the ally, the slave, the freed slave, the cousin, or the relation by marriage, as Ibn al-Atheer explains.

In addition to the fact that the hadith of Prophet Muhammad (sws) contains nothing about the issue of the imamate or what would indicate the caliphate, or whether Prophet Muhammad (sws) meant the caliphate, how would it seem better to use a word that would include all of the meanings we listed, instead of just stating it directly, as in: "Ali is my caliph after me," or "Ali is the imam after me," or "If I die, listen to and obey Ali ibn Abi Talib," so that there would be no disagreement, controversy, or dissent?!![37]

Why (if what the Shia say is true) didn't Prophet Muhammad (sws) use the word, "*wali*," instead of the word, "*mawla*," since the word, "*wali*," refers to the succession and rule, while the word, "*mawla*," refers to love and support??[38]

Prophet Muhammad (sws) did not use any of these definitive words.

So what do the Shia mean with this claim??

We conclude with an important explanation, which is:

According to the Words of Allah Almighty,

﴿إِنَّمَا وَلِيُّكُمُ اللَّهُ وَرَسُولُهُ وَالَّذِينَ آمَنُوا الَّذِينَ يُقِيمُونَ الصَّلَاةَ وَيُؤْتُونَ الزَّكَاةَ وَهُمْ رَاكِعُونَ﴾

It means, {**Verily, your *Wali* is Allah, His Messenger, and the believers, those who offer prayers perfectly, and give *zakat*** (poor due), **and they bow down.**}
[Al-Ma'idah 5: 55]

Allah Almighty is our *Mawla*, His messenger (sws) is a *mawla* for us, and the believers who establish the prayer and pay the *zakat*—among whom is Ali ibn Abi Talib—are each a *wali* for us.[39]

Consequently, we can see the enormity of the Shia's lies, half-truths, and slanderous accusations, as well as the egregious inventions with which they try to sow dissension in the ranks of Muslims, as a plot against Islam, out of hatred for its people.

6. The Shia found what they wanted (in terms of false interpretation) in some of the hadiths of Prophet Muhammad (sws), and they therefore invented the innovation of the twelve imams.

To explain the falseness of what the Shia claimed, we first mention some of the hadiths of Prophet Muhammad (sws) that the Shia focus on to get what they want, which go as follows:

A. The Messenger of Allah (sws) said,

«يكون اثنا عشر أميرًا كلهم من قريش»

It means, "[There will] **be twelve emirs** (leaders/princes), **all of them from Quraysh.**"[40]

B. The Messenger of Allah (sws) said,

«لا يزال الإسلام عزيزًا إلى اثني عشر خليفة كلهم من قريش»

It means, "**Islam will remain glorious until twelve caliphs, all of them from Quraysh.**"[41]

---

[37] *Huqbah min al-Taareekh*—with minor editing—by Shaikh Uthman al-Khamees
[38] Ibid.
[39] Ibid.
[40] Sahih al-Bukhari and Muslim
[41] Related by Muslim

C. The Messenger of Allah (sws) said,

«لا يزال هذا الدين عزيزًا منيعًا إلى اثني عشر رجلًا»

It means, "**This religion will remain glorious and unconquerable up till twelve men.**"⁴²

D. The Messenger of Allah (sws) said,

«لا يزال الدين قائمًا حتى يكون عليهم اثنا عشر خليفة كلهم تجتمع عليهم الأمة»

It means, "**The religion will remain standing until twelve caliphs have** [ruled] **over them, and the nation will be united on all of them.**"⁴³

To explain: It is from Allah Almighty's humiliation of this renegade sect (the Shia) that the hadiths of Prophet Muhammad (sws) (since they find what they want in the ability to interpret falsely) which they take as proof are, in fact, marked evidence of the reprehensibility of their message and the fallacious nature of their doctrines. Examples of this are:

In all of the previous hadiths mentioned, Prophet Muhammad (sws) explains that the true, unadulterated religion of Islam will remain glorious and unconquerable, since Allah Almighty made it appear and made its message victorious, passing through the caliphate of the first successor of Allah's Messenger (sws) (Abu Bakr al-Siddiq), then the second caliph (Umar ibn al-Khattab), then the third caliph (Uthman ibn `Affan), followed by the fourth caliph (Ali ibn Abi Talib), and then until the twelfth caliph.

However, the Shia, whose beliefs were founded on attacking the companions of Allah's Messenger (sws), have denied and contradicted what Prophet Muhammad (sws) said, declaring that the religion was not glorious during the period before Ali ibn Abi Talib's caliphate.

Undoubtedly, that is a total lie and an egregious affront, and it contradicts clear, straightforward hadiths of Prophet Muhammad (sws).

In fact, the historical events which took place during the time of the first successor to Allah's Messenger (sws) (Abu Bakr al-Siddiq), followed by the second caliph (Umar ibn al-Khattab), and then the third caliph (Uthman ibn `Affan), in terms of victories, the liberation of new lands, and the glory of Islam, which testify to the falseness of what the Shia claim and have taken as their doctrine.

It also shows:

The description of the twelve emirs or caliphs mentioned by Prophet Muhammad (sws) is as follows:

A. He will assume the caliphate.
B. Islam will be glorious during his era.
C. The people will be united under his caliphate.

None of the conditions explained by Allah's Messenger (sws) in his hadiths can be applied to any of those claimed by the Shia to be their imam.⁴⁴

Additionally, Prophet Muhammad (sws) declared these noble hadiths openly, letting his companions and his nation after him know about them.

However, what the Shia have claimed about their so-called imams is that:

Their succession was secretive, in that they say that Allah told the Angel Gabriel about the succession secretly, and Gabriel told Muhammad about it secretly, and Muhammad

---

⁴² Related by Muslim
⁴³ Related by Abu Dawud and al-Tabarani in *Al-Kabeer*
⁴⁴ *Huqbah min al-Taareekh*—with minor editing—by Shaikh Uthman al-Khamees

told Ali about it secretly, and Ali told whom he wanted about it secretly[45]...and so on, according to their claims and fabrications.

Additionally:
Al-Hassan al-Askari, whom the Shia claim to be their eleventh imam, died without descendants, so therefore, where is their twelfth imam?!

If the Shia have made up an imaginary, fantastic story about him (the twelfth imam, who in reality does not exist), then that would be contrary to reality—a type of mind trick—to bewilder the slightest degree of rationality.

Around the type we have mentioned briefly—the misconceptions the Shia have invented and stirred up—revolve the rest of the vile and trivial misconceptions they make up, which are not believable in the least, since the Shia rely, as we have shown, on unauthentic, non-authoritative hadiths, and they take and leave whatever they want from the verses and sayings of the Messenger (sws) according to what will conform with their false interpretations and wicked plans.

However, as we have shown, the result of all of this is humiliation and scandal for them at the hand of sincere scholars who have sold themselves for Allah (Glorious & Exalted), raising the banner of truth and inviting others to it, while exposing falsehood and warning others about it.

So, all praise is due to Allah Almighty for the blessing of Islam and for making us among the followers of the Sunnah of our beloved prophet, Muhammad (sws).

And all praise is due to Allah Almighty for the gift of guidance and righteousness.

---

[45] *Huqbah min al-Taareekh*—with minor editing—by Shaikh Uthman al-Khamees

Falsehood and Its Many Faces,
and How They Ally with One Another

To start, we should explain:
There are many falsehoods, and they ally themselves with one another, which is how it has many faces—the many faces of darkness.

Truth, on the other hand, is but one; it cannot get along with any of the faces of falsehood.

Truth is like light: with it, Allah Almighty erases the darknesses. Examples of this are as follows:

Take, for example, the thief and the murderer, the alcoholic, the fornicator, the devourer of interest...and those of a similar stripe; many relationships bring them together, springing from the camaraderie and intermingling of one with the other. Therefore, it is not strange to find them in different meetings, all coming together.

However, in the example of the pure, righteous person—who knows Allah's Rights, the eminence of His Messenger (sws), and the exemplary nature and application of the injunctions of his religion—when would he cross paths with those previously mentioned: (the thief, murderer, alcoholic, fornicator, devourer of interest...) or those of that sort? When would any relationship spring forth from familiarity and mutual affection between the one and the other? We would never find that.

Were we to witness a meeting between him and any of them, their souls would quickly be alienated and repel one another, and the explanation for that meeting would be that perhaps it was a temporary situation forced by one reason or another.

Also (may Allah Almighty be exalted), we find that this falsehood in all its different faces may gather its people (the followers of falsehood: the murderer, the thief...) in one common cell.

If someone was imprisoned because of his commitment and adherence to his religion and the Sunnah and example of his prophet (sws) or his rebellion because of a truth he holds fast to, that would be at the hands of those in power who act as enemies of Islam and its people, and he would not be thrown together with the followers of falsehood (the thief, murderer, etc.) in one common cell; rather, he (and those of his kind) would be in their own cell, separate from them.

Here we will sum up what we have said and turn to what we would like to get out of this and shed light upon, which is:

The Shia, with their false doctrines and the corrupt allegations they harbor, join with the Jews in secretive, clandestine relations (and there is nothing strange about that since, as we have pointed out, it was established by Abdullah ibn Saba', the Jew), as they also meet furtively with militant Christians in secret relations and hidden collusion, as well as with other non-Muslim groups. This is all a plot against Islam, out of hatred for its people who are the adherents of the Sunnah of our beloved prophet, Muhammad (sws).

Consequently, when the open enemies of Islam find such an ally (as the Shia and those of their ilk), would they let them go without reaping the benefits to be gained from them?! Would they waste such an opportunity when it is right between their hands?!

Answer: Of course not.

What we have shown here clearly explains the lack of advancement of these countries—which ally themselves against Islam and plot against it (the United States of America, Britain, and others)—towards Iran (which is populated by Shia for the most part) and the failure of their military program (and the like), and that is so that they can be an agent of the destruction of Islam and a thorn in the side of its people who are the adherents of the Sunnah of our beloved prophet, Muhammad (sws). The plans they have in common, and their goals are one (to plot against Islam and its people, those who are the people of the Sunnah of our beloved, Prophet Muhammad, sws).

The complete opposite is the case when, if these countries (enemies of Islam) saw the emergence of the true light of Islam at the hands of its people who hold fast to the Sunnah of their beloved and their prophet, Muhammad (sws), and his example, we would find them racing to put out their fire and root them out, but Allah Almighty refuses not to let His Light be fulfilled, even though the disbelievers and followers of falsehood hate it.

Among the testimony to this fact is:

- The Shia were the ones who helped the Tatars against the Muslims, and they were the reason the lands of Islam fell into their hands, to suffer the ruin and destruction of their homes and the slaughter and murder of their people. And history bears witness to that fact.
- The Shia are the ones who conspired with the Americans to bring down Afghanistan and make them fall under the occupation of the United States of America.
- The Shia are the ones who conspired with the Americans to bring down Iraq and to also fall under the occupation of the United States of America.

The Shia do not find any shame in confessing to that. They say:

If it weren't for Iran, neither Kabul (the capital of Afghanistan) nor Baghdad (the capital of Iraq) would have fallen, and by this, they mean into the hands of the Americans.

And there are more examples of the Shia allying themselves with the enemies of Islam, in the scope of clandestine relations and hidden collusions, to plot against Islam and its people.

That is to be expected when the founder of Shiism was Ibn Saba', the Jew.

Contrary to the Shia and their collaboration with the disbelievers and atheists to plot against Islam and to rip it out from the roots, we find the adherents of the Sunnah of the beloved, Prophet Muhammad (sws), refusing but to support Islam and raise high its flag.

As a result, what the people of Islam want contradicts what the enemies of Islam (Jews, militant Christians, and atheists) want.

Therefore, there are no common plans or secret machinations between the people of Islam (the adherents of the Sunnah of the beloved, Prophet Muhammad, sws) and those enemies.

Could raising the flag of Islam and holding high the banner of *tawhid* (the true Islamic monotheism of the adherents of the Sunnah of the beloved, Prophet Muhammad, sws) ever agree with the goal of those who wish to put out the Light of Allah Almighty, to plot and scheme against Islam, and to lower its flag?!!

Can truth agree with falsehood?!

Answer: Of course not, for truth is but one; it cannot agree with falsehood, all of which is darkness. For the truth is the light with which Allah Almighty erases all darknesses.

A Letter from the Adherents of the Sunnah of the Beloved, Prophet Muhammad (sws), to the Shia

The short, simple research this book contains includes part of the beliefs on which Shiism was founded, and therefore, our brief message addressed to those who follow the Shia way consists of what we will relate in the following manner:

To begin: We (the adherents of the Sunnah of the beloved, Prophet Muhammad, sws) would like them (the Shia) not to hold anything in themselves against us for the truth of matters we have elucidated herein so that the truth may prevail and that falsehood may be defeated.

Second: We (the adherents of the Sunnah of the beloved, Prophet Muhammad, sws) invite them (the Shia) to discard any partisanship, fanaticism, or nationalism...and anything else of the sort, only for the sake of Allah Almighty, while reading such a short, simple study or any other valuable book which may clarify at length the truth of the matter and distinguish correct from faulty beliefs, while providing a full and comprehensive refutation of anything related to the doubts stirred up by these misconceptions.

Third: We (the adherents of the Sunnah of the beloved, Prophet Muhammad, sws) invite them (the Shia) to use and employ well the gifts and blessings we have been granted by Allah Almighty, especially the gift of reason, and to distinguish thereby between the correct and the faulty and between the decent and the inferior by means of simple questions, as follows:

Which beliefs does the sound, straightforward mind approve? And which ideas can it accept? Which doctrines are better?

Which beliefs do not conflict with it (with straightforward reason)?

With which beliefs and ideas does the mind not find any contradiction?

And so on with questions of this type ...

Fourth: We (the adherents of the Sunnah of the beloved, Prophet Muhammad, sws) invite them (the Shia) to return to the nature Allah Almighty created them with when they were born (for every child is born with a sound nature, or *fitrah*) before the alteration and manipulation happened, and this, through some simple questions, as follows:

Which beliefs and ideas would someone of sound human nature and a pure soul approve?

Which beliefs and ideas would someone of sound human nature and a pure soul not find the least objection to?

In which beliefs and ideas would someone find the pure, sound nature he was first created with—that of pure monotheism and complete veneration of Allah (Glorious & Exalted)?

And so on with questions of this type...

Fifth: We (the adherents of the Sunnah of the beloved, Prophet Muhammad, sws) invite them (the Shia), if the truth mixes with their tender hearts, not to fear before Allah the censure of any critic. We invite them to be determined to follow the truth which Allah Almighty has led them to, to have patience with what they may face from other Shia on account of their following him or their attachment to him, that they do not find in themselves any difficulty in abandoning falsehood (which their fathers and grandfathers were upon) and renouncing it, seeking help in that from Allah Almighty, and then from those whom He (Glorious & Exalted) guides to help him and lead him to His path.

Sixth: We (the adherents of the Sunnah of the beloved, Prophet Muhammad, sws) invite them (the Shia), after they know the path of truth, to walk it, and to proceed in calling others to it, thanking Allah Almighty for the great gift of being guided to Him and to the

Sunnah of His beloved and chosen one, Muhammad (sws), hoping for others to be guided to Allah (Blessed & Most High), and taking whatever steps in that they are able to.

Seventh: We (the adherents of the Sunnah of the beloved, Prophet Muhammad, sws) would like to let them (the Shia) know that, just as Allah (Blessed & Exalted) guided us to Him and to the example of His beloved and His prophet, Muhammad (sws) and to follow his Sunnah, we do not dislike for anyone else to be granted this blessing; on the contrary, we would like everyone to be guided to Him, so we ask Allah (Glorious & Exalted) to bring His slaves back to Him in a beautiful, gentle way, and to guide them to Him and to the Sunnah of His beloved and His prophet, Muhammad (sws), with a guidance that will not be led astray again.

This is what we wished our message (that of the adherents of the Sunnah of the beloved, Prophet Muhammad, sws) to say to the Shia, after examining what we have included in this brief study, explaining the facts and exposing falsehood, by way of raising some questions to help in that respect.

And we ask Allah Almighty to make us rightly-guided and to guide others through us.

Conclusion

We have indicated, in the preceding points, part of what the Shia doctrines contain which proves them to be false, but many people are not aware of what the Shia (and those of their ilk) believe, from the likes of what we have mentioned of false allegations and abominable accusations that no one of untarnished nature, pure soul, and sound mind could believe to be right, and Allah Almighty and His Messenger (sws) are innocent of them. As such, these simpleminded people have been deceived by the idea of Shiism under the cover of the dissimulation (*taqiya*) the Shia are so skilled at. So these simple people have taken Shia beliefs as their doctrine and way of life, concealing the opposite of what they reveal with sweet words and lovely actions, becoming their chosen prey and being used by the Shia due to their ignorance and lack of awareness of the truth of the matter.

Therefore, we, the adherents of the Sunnah of the beloved, Prophet Muhammad (sws), must not spare any effort to raise the awareness of these simple people, who have been duped so easily by what this renegade sect are upon, especially in this age—the age of satellite television and the Internet—since the Shia broadcast their venom and misconceptions over their own special channels, and even under cover of some of the (misguided) Sufi groups, secretly, so that their actions are not exposed and their plans do not fail. (The spread of Shia beliefs is an important issue due to the continued existence of the illegal and brutal Zionist entity and the protection thereof, as it was important before due to the presence of the Crusaders. As such, among that which Salahuddin al-Ayoubi did through his successful efforts and blessed attempts to defend Islam and the Muslims by getting rid of the false Shia *madhhab* (school of jurisprudence) which cooperated with the plans of the enemies of Islam—since the founder of that corrupt *madhhab* was Ibn Saba', the Jew, as we have shown before—and as a result, Salahuddin al-Ayoubi was able, by the Grace of Allah Almighty, to unite the lands and get rid of the Crusaders and their oppression.)

It is therefore imperative that we do not let ourselves be carried away by this deceptive media which falsifies facts (and the clear proof of that is plentiful), which displays lies as though the Shia (and those of their ilk) were at odds with that so-called Zionist entity (Israel), and those who support it, such as the United States of America, in order to complete the plan to spread the beliefs of the Shia, who hate the followers of the best of humankind, Muhammad (sws), since they conquered the lands of Persia and put an end to their empire, and spread the correct example of Islam and the pure Sunnah of His Prophet, Muhammad (sws) and its laws, so that they might find acceptance through the lies spread about its conflict (the Shia doctrines) with the so-called Zionist entity and its supporters, but the clear truth is as we have explained, which is:

The spread of Shia beliefs is a crucial issue due to the continued presence of that illegal and brutal Zionist entity and the protection of it, just as it was crucial before, due to the presence of the Crusaders (in the Arab World), because of their common purpose of ripping this religion (Islam) out by the roots, as well as those who hold fast to it and follow the Sunnah of its prophet, Muhammad (sws): the adherents of the Sunnah of the beloved, Prophet Muhammad (sws).

Ahlus-Sunnah, especially its scholars, therefore, must raise the banner of knowledge, expending all their efforts and power, to use and employ to the best of their abilities the modern technological means at their disposal (especially satellite television and the Internet), to explain the truth and defeat falsehood; to explain what this misguided, renegade sect (the Shia and those of their ilk) are about in terms of their reprehensible message and corrupt beliefs; to explain the vile misconceptions they stir up and produce a comprehensive refutation of them; and to explain the secret agendas and vicious schemes that exist between them and the enemies of Islam to plot against Islam and its people, and so on.

As a result, we could then bring about the downfall of falsehood and erase it, for truth is clear and bright, while falsehood is repetitive, and falsehood cannot, with all the darkness in it, continue if the light of truth and its luminance gain power over it.

In conclusion, we would like to raise a few salient questions, after explaining the difference between truth and falsehood, and they are as follows:

What is acceptable to those of untainted human nature and pure souls, who are fully devoted to Allah (Blessed & Most High)??

What would those of sound, righteous minds accept when they would accept no other??

Is it the beliefs of the Shia (and those of their ilk), of which we have shown part of their reprehensibility, since they are based on: defamation of the Divine Creator (Glorious & Exalted)—as in the Doctrine of *Bada'* and others—and hatred of one of the angels (in fact, the best of them, who is the Trustworthy Gabriel, peace be upon him, who was entrusted with bringing down the Revelation from on high to the prophets and messengers), denying what in in the Holy Quran (the Seal of the Divine Scriptures and the great miracle of Prophet Muhammad, sws), and claiming it has been corrupted, and which is based on attacking the honor of Allah's Messenger (sws)—by accusing the Mother of the Believers, Aisha, may Allah be pleased with her, of adultery), and which is based on insulting and cursing the noble companions (may Allah be pleased with them all)—when they are the ones who aided the Messenger (sws) and supported his mission—and which is based on sexual permissiveness by way of a type of 'marriage' prohibited by Allah Almighty and His Messenger (sws), known as *mut`a* marriage, and which is based on taking people's money wrongfully (through the so-called *Khums* for the hidden imam), and which is based on heresy and idolatry (as in the Shia exaggeration with the so-called imams at whose graves they call upon them for help)...in addition to the other fabrications and allegations whose falsehood we have explained herein which contradict untainted human nature as well as the slightest degree of logic? **Or is it the beliefs of the adherents of the Sunnah of the beloved, Prophet Muhammad (sws)**, with their clear, pure beliefs, without blemish or murkiness, since they are: based on veneration of Allah (Glorious & Exalted) and belief in the Perfection of His Attributes; based on faith in all the angels without diminishing their status, and that the best of them and the most noble is Gabriel (peace be upon him), the Guardian of Heavenly Revelation, who was entrusted with the Divine Message; based on faith in the Holy Quran and its protection by Allah (Blessed & Most High) until the Day of Judgment; based on love for the members of Prophet Muhammad's (sws) chosen and noble household and knowledge of their status, including the wives of Prophet Muhammad (sws), among whom is Aisha (may Allah be pleased with her), the Mother of the Believers, whose innocence of the liars' accusation Allah Almighty declared from above the seven heavens, and therefore, the honor of the best of the messengers, Muhammad (sws); based on reverence for the noble companions (may Allah be pleased with them all) and knowledge of their rights and virtues (for they were the first to believe in Allah's Messenger, sws, aid him, and support him until his mission and message spread, then they carried the banner of this great religion to the ends of the known world, east and west, north and south); based on prohibition of fornication and sexual permissiveness by forbidding what Allah and His Messenger (sws) prohibited, known as *mut`a* marriage; based on not devouring other people's money wrongfully; based on complete *tawhid*, pure monotheism, making their worship for Allah (Glorious & Exalted) Alone, and therefore, contradicting the Shia and others in their heresy and idolatry; and based on (the belief of the adherents of the Sunnah of the beloved, Prophet Muhammad, sws) agreement with pure, untainted human nature and straightforward, sound logic??!

The answer about which there can be no neutrality, alternative, or controversy is that:

Pure, sound human nature, purified, righteous souls, which are singularly devoted to Allah Almighty, and wise, rightly-guided minds cannot accept anything but what the adherents of the Sunnah of Prophet Muhammad (sws) are upon, in terms of pure and clear beliefs, which contain no blemish or murkiness; they cannot accept anything other than that at all.

We conclude this point with a question, the answer to which we will leave up to the reader, and it is as follows:

What responsibility do I bear as someone who worships only Allah and believes in the Seal of His Prophets and Messengers, Muhammad (sws), and in the Final Book revealed (the Holy Quran), if I gain the noble companions and win their love, without losing the chosen and pure family of Prophet Muhammad (sws) or neglecting their status and position?!!

So, all praise is due to Allah Almighty for the blessing of Islam, and for making us among the adherents of the Sunnah of the beloved, Muhammad (sws), and all praise is due to Allah Almighty for the gift of guidance and righteousness.

We ask Allah Almighty to guide us to the best of deeds and to help us in them. We ask Him to use us (the adherents of the Sunnah of the beloved, Prophet Muhammad, sws) to support His religion (Islam) while He is Well-Pleased with us. We ask Him to accept from us and from everyone, the rest of our deeds, to make them acceptable in this life and in the Hereafter, and to make them grow for us, for He (Blessed & Most High) is the Only One with the Authority over that and He is the Only One Capable of it.

And may Allah send peace and blessing on His beloved and His prophet, Muhammad (sws), upon the pure, noble members of his family, his noble companions, and all those who walk in his footsteps, imitate his example, and follow his guidance until the Day of Judgment.

And all praise is due to Allah, Lord of the Worlds.

www.ingramcontent.com/pod-product-compliance
Lightning Source LLC
LaVergne TN
LVHW020427080526
838202LV00055B/5062